The Basic Book of
Home Maintenance and Repair

T. J. Roybal and G. C. Edmondson

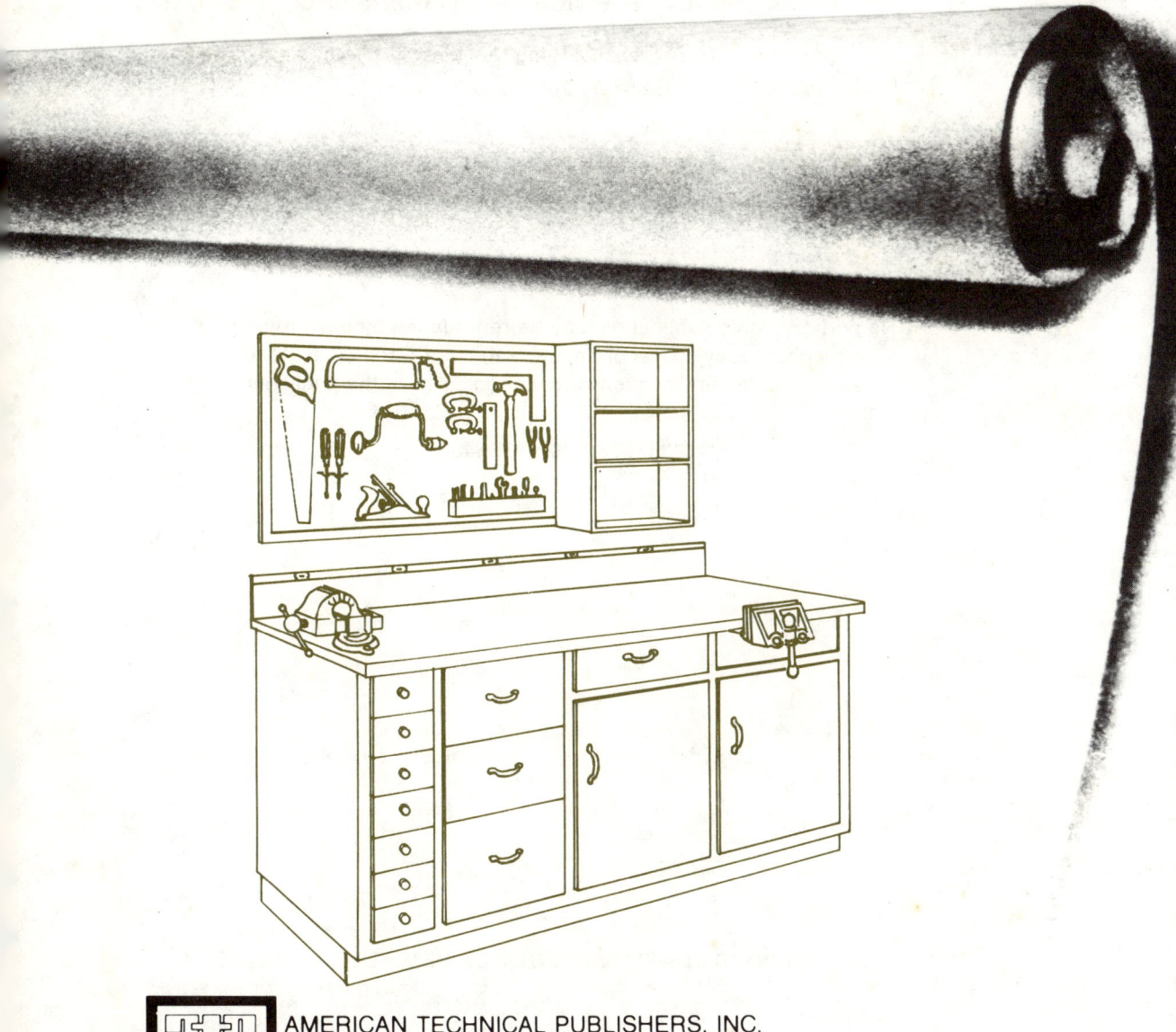

AMERICAN TECHNICAL PUBLISHERS, INC.
ALSIP, ILLINOIS 60658

COPYRIGHT© 1979

BY AMERICAN TECHNICAL PUBLISHERS, INC.

Library of Congress Catalog Number: 79-51403
ISBN: 0-8269-4410-8

No portion of this publication may be reproduced by any process such as photocopying, recording, storage in a retrieval system or transmitted by any means without permission of the publisher

123456789-79-98765432

PRINTED IN THE UNITED STATES OF AMERICA

CONTENTS

1 — page 1 Introduction

Unit 1	2	Safety
Unit 2	5	Tool Safety
Unit 3	6	Fasteners

2 — 9 Electricity

Unit 4	10	Electrical Safety
Unit 5	13	Electrical Plugs
Unit 6	15	Cords and Sockets
Unit 7	17	Outlets and Switches
Unit 8	21	Wire Splices
Unit 9	24	Doorbells
Unit 10	27	Fluorescent Lights
Unit 11	30	Meter Reading

3 — 32 Plumbing

Unit 12	33	Plumbing Safety
Unit 13	35	Faucets
Unit 14	38	Toilets
Unit 15	42	Pipes and Pipe Fittings
Unit 16	45	Joining Pipe and Tubing
Unit 17	48	Sink and Basin Traps
Unit 18	50	Sewer Pipes
Unit 19	52	Water Heaters
Unit 20	55	Heating and Air Conditioning

4 — 58 Finishing Walls

Unit 21	59	Ceiling and Walls
Unit 22	61	Wall Repairs
Unit 23	64	Paint Safety
Unit 24	67	Preparing Walls for Paint
Unit 25	69	Mixing Paint
Unit 26	71	Painting Methods
Unit 27	76	Wall Coverings
Unit 28	80	Paneling and Wood Trim

CONTENTS

5 — page 82 — Structural Maintenance

Unit 29	83	Floor Coverings
Unit 30	85	Window Frames
Unit 31	88	Glazing
Unit 32	91	Doors and Frames
Unit 33	93	Door Hardware
Unit 34	95	Roofs
Unit 35	99	Roofing Accessories

6 — 102 — Concrete and Asphalt

Unit 36	103	Mortar and Concrete
Unit 37	105	Masonry Repairs
Unit 38	107	Pouring Concrete
Unit 39	109	Basements

7 — 111 — Furniture Maintenance

Unit 40	112	Furniture Repair
Unit 41	115	Refinishing Furniture
Unit 42	117	Outdoor Furniture
	119	**Glossary**
	121	**Index**

PREFACE

THE BASIC BOOK OF HOME MAINTENANCE AND REPAIR is part of an integrated series of Industrial Arts textbooks designed to teach basic skills to beginning students. Its major objectives are: career exploration, and the development of consumer awareness, manipulative skills, and craftsmanship. The philosophy of THE BASIC BOOK OF HOME MAINTENANCE AND REPAIR is based on a recent, nationwide survey in which home maintenance teachers at all levels were asked to outline the courses they actually taught and let us know what types of instructional materials they needed. The result is a highly-visual text with a controlled reading level that will help insure student success.

The Publisher

INTRODUCTION   1

Suppose a broken water pipe is drowning your house upstairs. Downstairs the basement light switch doesn't work. The front door won't lock, and, whenever it rains, the kitchen window frames and floor are getting soaked.

Will you call a plumber, an electrician, a locksmith, and a glazier? These are specialists who fix faucets, wires, locks, and windows. Or, will you fix your house yourself?

Most homeowners know something about home maintenance and repair. They can't afford not to. It is too expensive to hire a professional everytime something goes wrong with a house.

In this course you can learn enough to fix faucets, lights, windows, and doors—and many more things besides. You will learn how things work. On a very difficult job, you may still have to call a specialist. But you will learn here to work with tools and make many repairs yourself. You will learn about carpentry, electricity, painting, plumbing and a dozen other trades. And, with practice, you can become good at all of them.

Unit 1   SAFETY

Every trade or craft has its own safety rules. Safety rules are simply common sense. They are intended to keep people from hurting themselves. Because home maintenance and repair people work with many different types of tools and materials, they need to know how to prevent accidents more than anyone else. Always remember:

- Tools will cut, stab, or hurt people only if they are handled carelessly
- Power tools must always be turned off when not in use
- Tools not in use should be put away
- Tools in bad condition may cause accidents
- Electricity is invisible. Assume it is present in every wire unless you have turned it off yourself and checked to make sure it is off
- Strange odors from chemicals or paint can injure and kill people
- Many cleaners and paint thinners will explode if exposed to fire or extreme heat
- Goggles protect eyes from chips thrown by tools
- Open flames must be turned off when not in use
- Neatness prevents accidents of all kinds

A number of tools (figure 1-1) are necessary for good repair work. Proper use of tools makes the work neater and more professional looking. Improper use of tools causes more accidents and injuries than any other kind of carelessness.

The basic safety rules for using any hand tools are:
- Use the right tool for the job
- Never use dull cutting tools
- Keep tools repaired
- Turn off electrical tools when not in use
- Make sure work being drilled or cut is properly clamped

Safety equipment such as goggles (figure 1-2) for eye protection and insulated gloves (figure 1-3) for working with hot objects like soldered tubing should be kept handy.

The most important safety rule to remember is to use common sense and think ahead. Don't unscrew a water pipe unless the water pressure is turned off. Cold water may ruin the house. Hot water may ruin you. Gas pipes are even more dangerous.

Keep in mind that a saw that will cut a four by four oak post can also cut off a finger. Flames used to melt lead will cook a careless hand. Something that dissolves paint may also dissolve skin!

SELF CHECK

1. Why shouldn't tools in poor condition be used?
2. What are things you can wear to help prevent accidents?
3. What should you do before you remove a water pipe?
4. What is the most important safety rule?

Safety 3

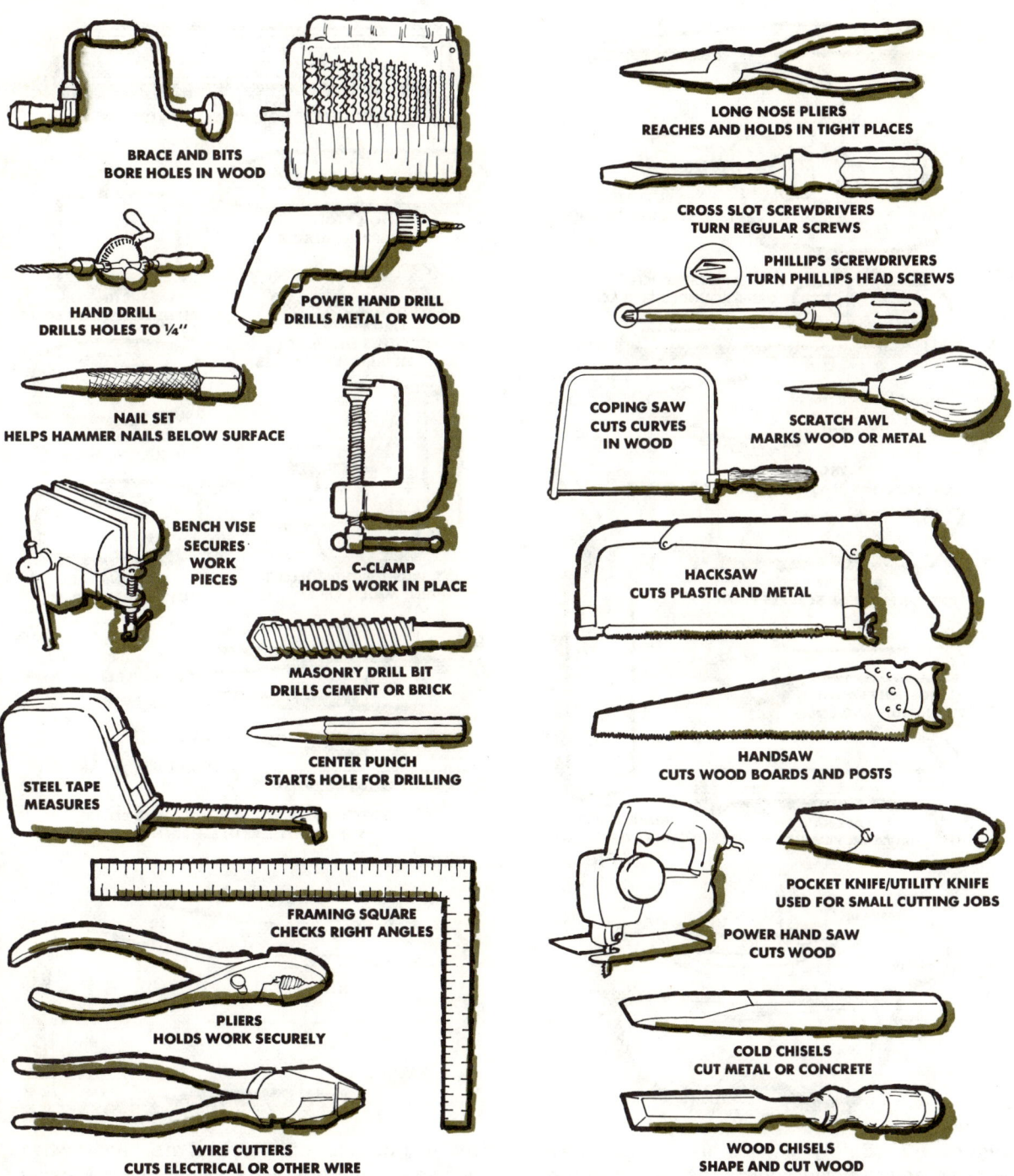

Figure 1-1: A good selection of tools is important for good work. Using the proper tool for each job prevents accidents and gives better results.

4 Home Maintenance and Repair

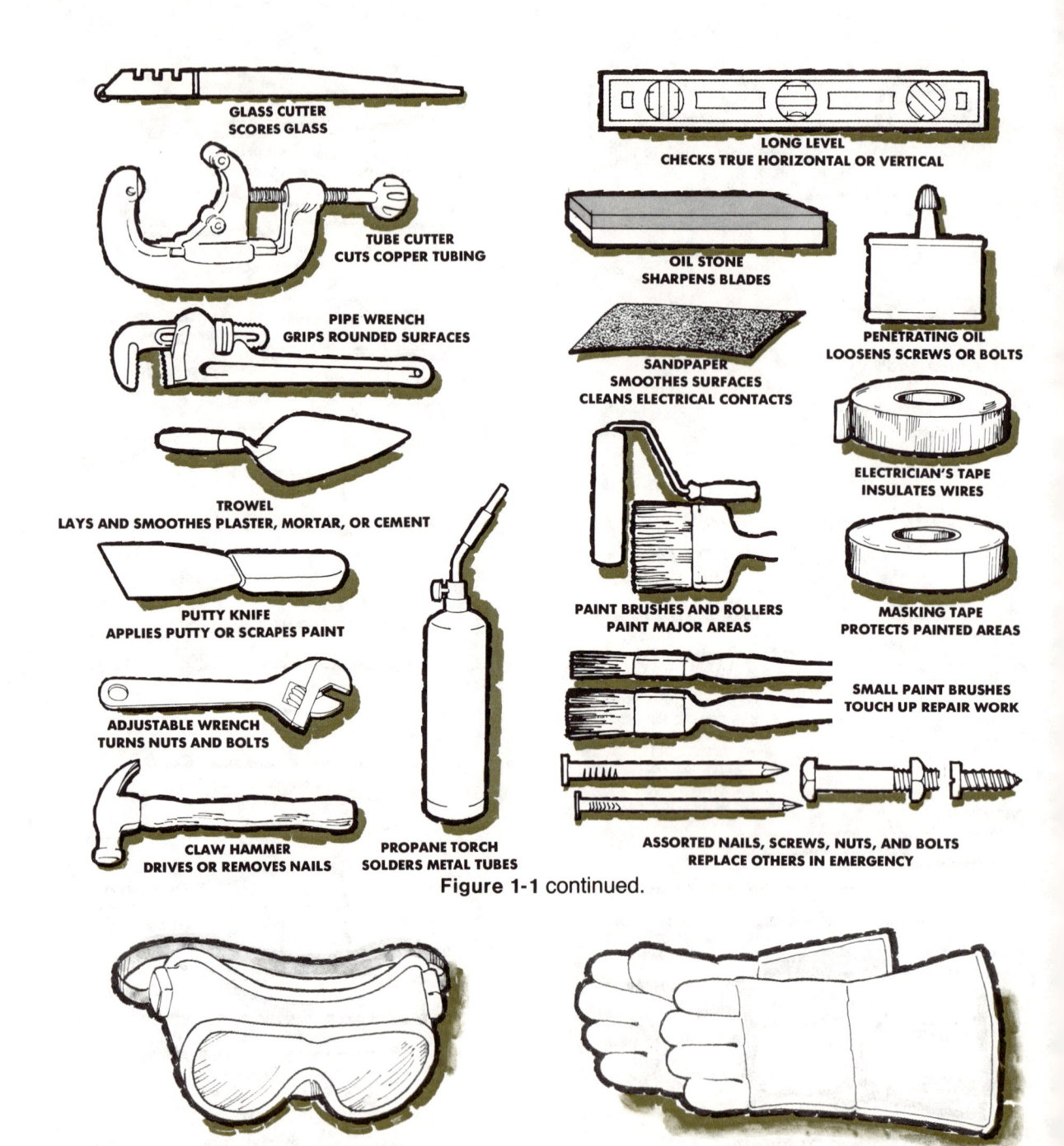

GLASS CUTTER SCORES GLASS

TUBE CUTTER CUTS COPPER TUBING

PIPE WRENCH GRIPS ROUNDED SURFACES

TROWEL LAYS AND SMOOTHES PLASTER, MORTAR, OR CEMENT

PUTTY KNIFE APPLIES PUTTY OR SCRAPES PAINT

ADJUSTABLE WRENCH TURNS NUTS AND BOLTS

CLAW HAMMER DRIVES OR REMOVES NAILS

PROPANE TORCH SOLDERS METAL TUBES

LONG LEVEL CHECKS TRUE HORIZONTAL OR VERTICAL

OIL STONE SHARPENS BLADES

SANDPAPER SMOOTHES SURFACES CLEANS ELECTRICAL CONTACTS

PENETRATING OIL LOOSENS SCREWS OR BOLTS

PAINT BRUSHES AND ROLLERS PAINT MAJOR AREAS

ELECTRICIAN'S TAPE INSULATES WIRES

MASKING TAPE PROTECTS PAINTED AREAS

SMALL PAINT BRUSHES TOUCH UP REPAIR WORK

ASSORTED NAILS, SCREWS, NUTS, AND BOLTS REPLACE OTHERS IN EMERGENCY

Figure 1-1 continued.

Figure 1-2: Safety glasses are necessary for working around power tools. They will also protect against dripping paint, sparks, or spattering chemicals.

Figure 1-3: Insulated gloves are handy when you work with hot water lines, tubing being soldered, or even electrical wires. But don't trust them to keep high voltage from injuring you.

TOOL SAFETY   Unit 2

By themselves, tools are not dangerous. Tools become dangerous only in the hands of a careless person. The best safety rules for handling tools are the simplest:
- Keep all tools in good condition (figure 2-1)
- Use the correct tool for the job
- Put away all tools when you are not using them (figure 2-2)
- Keep your working area neat and clean
- Know which end of a tool cuts, and always keep that end turned away

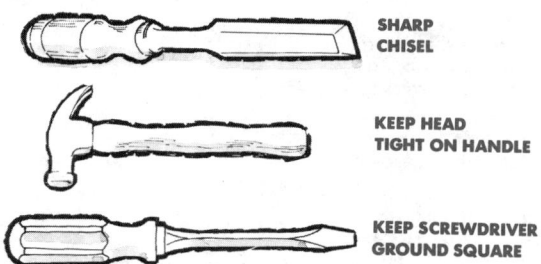

Figure 2-1: Tools in good shape are easier and safer to work with. Dull chisels, loose hammer heads, and broken screwdrivers should be repaired or replaced.

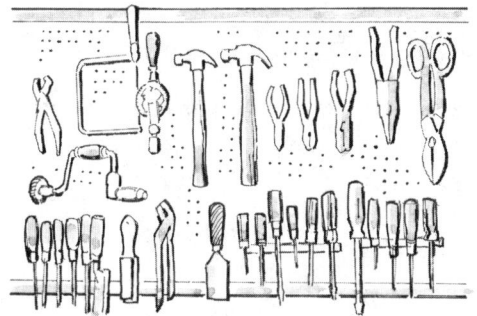

Figure 2-2: Tools that are safely put away do not cause accidents and injury.

Figure 2-3: Besides doing a better job, sharp tools are safer to use than dull tools. Sharp tools are less likely to slip. Always cut away from yourself or anyone else in the room.

from yourself and other people (figure 2-3)
- Use power tools that are grounded or double-insulated
- Wear eye protection when you use tools that make flying chips
- Keep power tool guards in place

People can stumble and fall on a sharp saw or chisel. They can accidentally knock a hammer off a bench on to someone's foot. If everything is put away, <u>all the time</u>, accidents like these become rare.

SELF CHECK

1. When are tools dangerous?
2. Why should cutting tools be kept sharp?
3. When should you wear eye protection?
4. What is the best way to avoid accidents?

Unit 3　　　　　　　　　FASTENERS

Everyone knows what a nail or a screw is—until a store clerk asks which kind you want. There are many to choose from (figure 3-1). The most common fasteners are:

- Tacks, nails, and brads
- Screws
- Nuts and bolts

Tacks have large heads. Brads are small nails. Nails are sized by the "penny" (d): the bigger the penny number, the larger the nail (figure 3-2). Some nails have extra-large heads to keep from pulling through soft material. Finish nails or casing nails have very small heads so they can be set

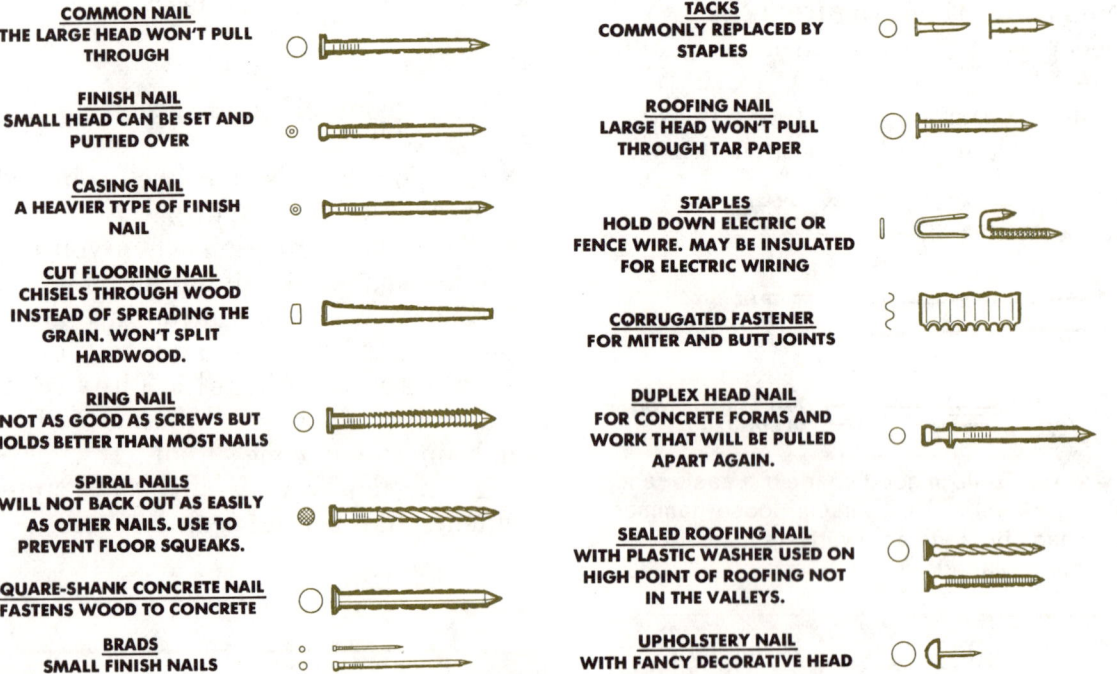

Figure 3-1: Most people don't realize how many kinds of nails there are or how many special uses they have.

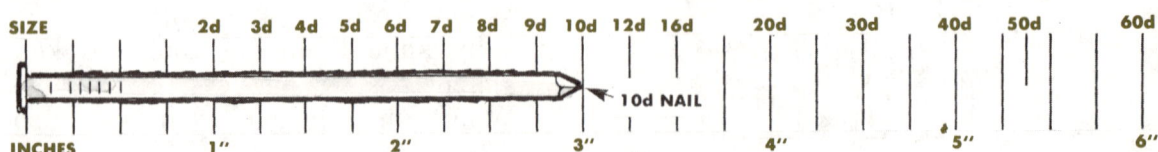

Figure 3-2: Nails are described in penny numbers. The d stands for penny, which refers to the size, not the price. The larger the penny number, the larger the nail is.

Fasteners 7

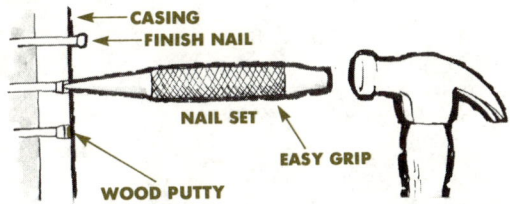

Figure 3-3: Finish nails are set so that they are not seen when the job is finished. Drive the nail in most of the way with a hammer. Stop before the hammer hits the surface. Choose the correct size nail set, place it on the nail, and continue driving the nail until it is below the surface. Finally fill the hole with wood putty.

below the surface. This is done with a nail set (figure 3-3). The holes are then puttied over. There are even special nails to be driven into concrete.

Screws also come in many types and sizes (figure 3-4). Their size is based on their length and the thickness of the shank. Screw gages (figure 3-5) tell how thick the shank is. Most screws with flat heads can be driven so they are flush with the surface. This is called countersinking (figure 3-6).

Figure 3-5: A screw gage will measure the thickness of the shank.

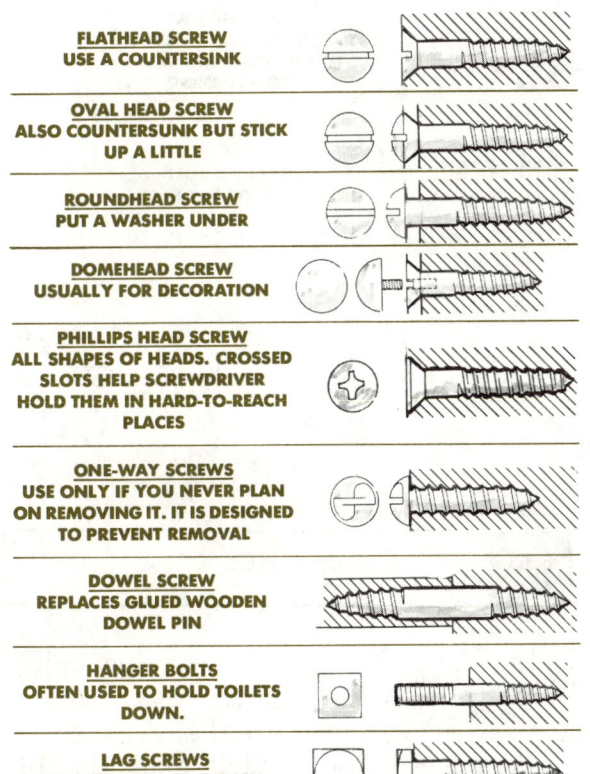

Figure 3-4: Screw types.

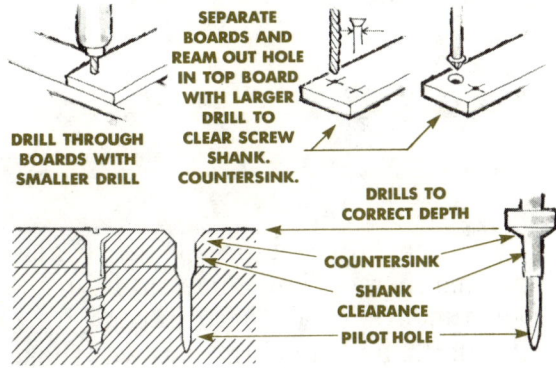

Figure 3-6: Countersinking and drilling for flathead screws. If you have to sink a large number of screws, buy a special bit that drills both size holes and countersinks all at once. A little wax rubbed on the screw thread will make it easy to drive the screw into the wood.

8 Home Maintenance and Repair

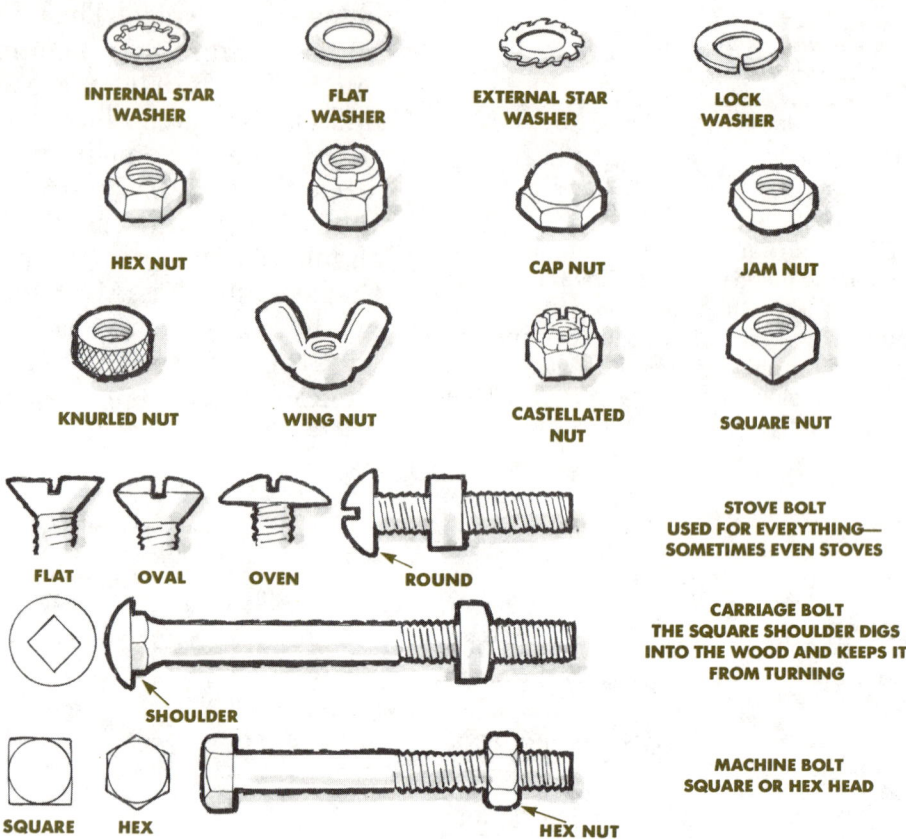

Figure 3-7: Nuts, bolts and washers.

Nuts and bolts (figure 3-7) are also good fasteners. They come in different sizes and are used for different jobs. Nuts, bolts, and machine screws (those used for metal) have a number telling the diameter of the shank, followed by another number which tells how many threads per inch. For example a 1/4-20 bolt has a 1/4 inch shank and 20 threads per inch.

SELF CHECK

1. Is a 5d nail larger than a 10d nail?
2. What is a finish nail?
3. How do you use a nail set?
4. In a 3/8-16 bolt, what does the 16 mean?

ELECTRICITY   2

In this age of electricity, modern homes have more and more electricity built into them. In home maintenance and repair, knowledge about electricity is a must. It is important to know which electrical jobs you can handle and when to call an electrician.

People who work with electricity are called electricians. As specialists, they put wires in houses, install fuse boxes or panels, repair large electrical appliances, work on doorbells, and generally handle all common electrical equipment problems.

The most common house current is 110 volt, 60 hertz per second alternating current (called AC). AC is a type of electricity that "alternates." This means that it changes its direction of flow as it passes through a wire. Sixty hertz AC is electricity that changes its direction of flow 60 times each second.

Another current, 220 volt AC is also available for use in most homes. It is very dangerous to work with, and a qualified electrician should be called in

if you suspect trouble in a 220 volt circuit.

Electricity may be dangerous, but it is not difficult to work with if you follow certain basic rules. The following units include the basic safety rules for working with electricity and explain simple electrical repairs you can make around the house.

Unit 4   ELECTRICAL SAFETY

When speaking of electricity, the word hot means charged with electricity. Hot also means dangerous. To avoid danger when working with electricity, follow these rules:
- Assume that all electrical wires and parts are hot
- Always check to make sure that the electricity is turned off before starting or continuing any electrical work
- Never turn on the electricity for someone else unless asked to do so
- Always check for electricity with a circuit tester
- Never work with wires or electrical equipment in wet or damp places

Electricity is invisible. You can't tell if a wire is hot by looking at it. Things that electricity can run through are called conductors. Things that electricity cannot run through are called insulators. Electricity runs well through most metals and through water. So wires and electrical parts are made of metal. Because the human body is mostly water, it also makes a good conductor of electricity. Always be careful around electricity!

When you are working with appliances, you can turn off the electricity by pulling the plug (figure 4-1). Most shop work is done this way. But when you are working on wiring in a house you must turn off the electricity in a different way.

Figure 4-1: Be safe when working with electricity. Pull the plug and keep it in sight so someone will not plug it in again while you are working. Make sure you have pulled the right plug.

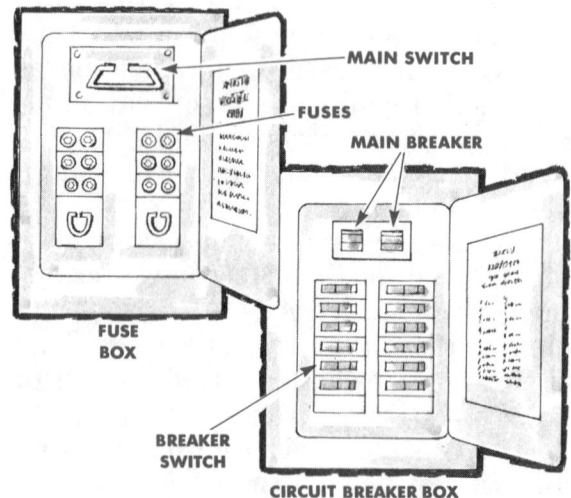

Figure 4-2: The fuse box or breaker switch box is where electricity enters the house. Turning electricity off at the box makes house wiring safe to work on.

Electrical Safety 11

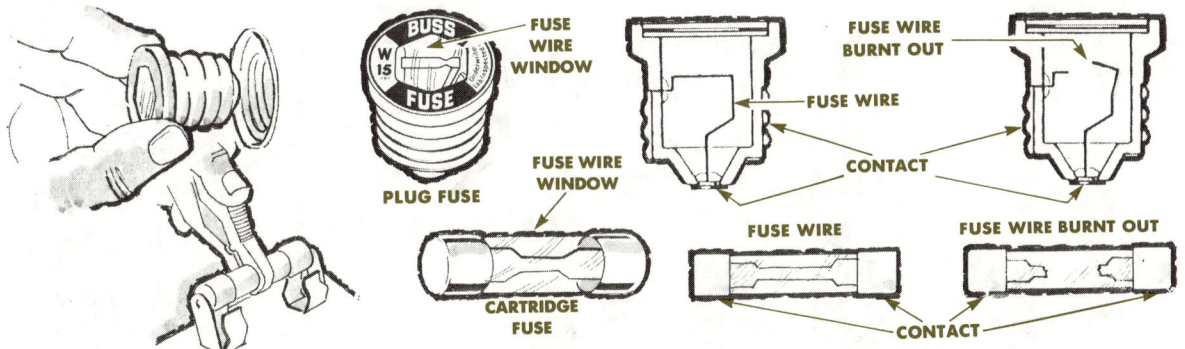

Figure 4-3: Fuses are designed to melt and break the circuit when the flow of electricity becomes too great. Removing the fuse will also break the circuit.

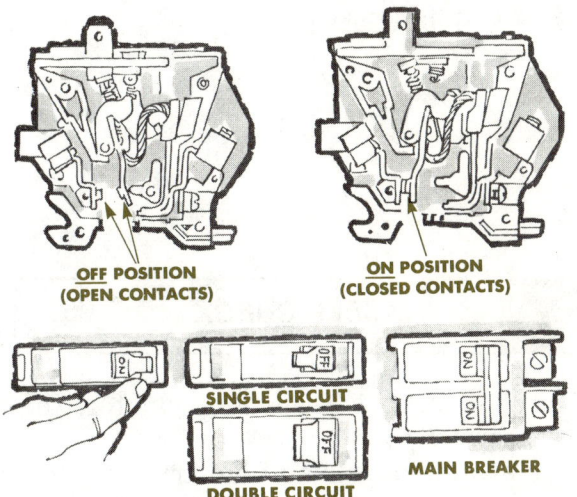

Figure 4-4: Blown fuses must be replaced. Blown circuit breakers, however, may be reset by hand.

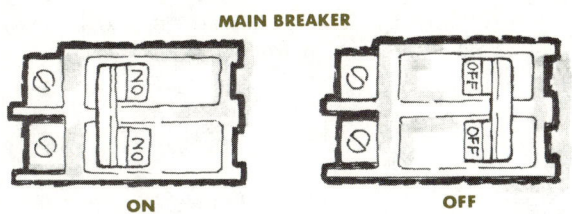

Figure 4-5: The main switch on a fuse or circuit breaker box controls all the electricity in the house.

All house wiring runs to a fuse box or breaker box (figure 4-2). A fuse or breaker in this box completes each circuit. Too much electricity flowing through a wire could make it hot enough to melt and cause a fire. To prevent this, the fuse (figure 4-3) will melt or the circuit breaker (figure 4-4) will open automatically when the wires get too hot. This opens the circuit and stops the flow of electricity. The electricity can also be stopped by removing the fuse or opening the circuit breaker by hand.

The circuit breaker box and the fuse box have a main switch (figure 4-5). This switch turns on or off all the electricity in the house. When electricians are working they will padlock the main switch in the off position and tag it (figure 4-6).

A careful electrician tests bare wires with a circuit tester. A circuit tester (figure 4-7) is made of two wire probes and a small bulb which glows if electricity is flowing through the wire being checked.

12 Home Maintenance and Repair

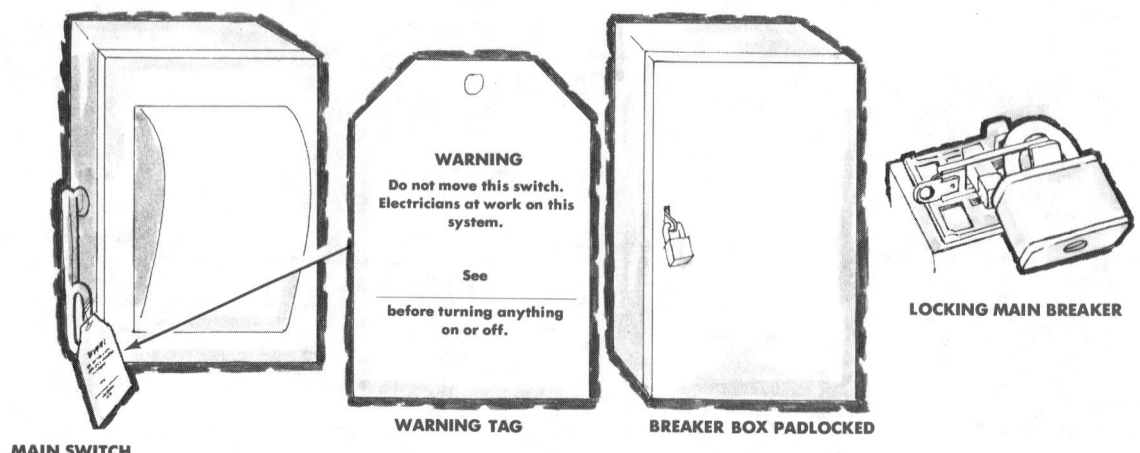

Figure 4-6: On fuse boxes the switch may be locked open to insure that the electricity remains off. On circuit breaker boxes, the main switch is thrown and the cover is then locked.

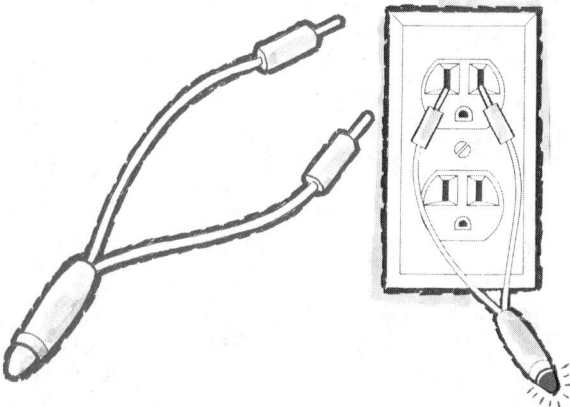

Figure 4-7: Most circuit testers are made of two wires or probes and a neon bulb. The two probes are touched to the wires. If the bulb glows, the wires are hot (electricity is flowing). Circuit testers have different voltage ratings so be sure you are using the correct type.

SELF CHECK

1. What are two good conductors of electricity?
2. How do you turn off electricity when you are going to work on an appliance?
3. How does a fuse work?
4. What is the best way to test that electricity has been turned off?

ELECTRICAL PLUGS   Unit 5

When appliances don't work properly, the plug is often the problem. Prongs may be broken or bent. Wires may be burnt where they attach to the prongs. The plug itself may be split or cracked (figure 5-1).

There are two basic types of plugs:
- Clamp-on plugs
- Wired plugs

Clamp-on plugs (figure 5-2) are easiest to replace. They have no screws and require no stripping. Cut off the damaged plug, and separate the wires for about 1/4 inch. Open the clamp or lever on the new plug and simply insert the wire ends into the plug. Close the clamp or lever, and the plug is ready for use. Clamp-on plugs should be used only for light-duty use, such as lamp cords.

To repair a wired plug (figure 5-3) take out the cardboard or plastic cover and loosen the screws. Pull the wires farther through the plug and cut off the bad ends. Separate the two wires for about 1-1/2 inches and strip 1/2 inch of insulation off the ends (figure 5-4). Twist the copper strands so they will not separate easily. To relieve the stress on the plug and on the copper wire, tie an "underwriters knot" as shown in figure 5-5.

Pull the knot back into the plug cap and wrap the bare wire ends around the screws in the direction the screw tightens (figure 5-6). Tighten the screws and replace the cover.

If your plug has three prongs (figure 5-7) repair it the same as a two-prong

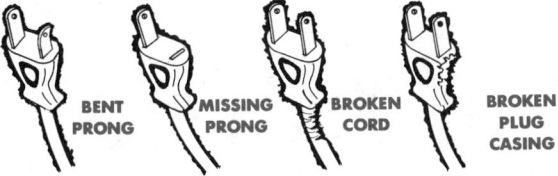

Figure 5-1: Broken electrical plugs are often the cause of appliance failure. Plugs are frequently stepped on or kicked accidentally. Common damage includes bent and broken prongs, broken or burnt wires, and damaged plug casings.

Figure 5-2: This clamp-on type plug is easily installed. The lever is opened and the wires inserted. As the lever is closed, sharp points within the plug pierce the wire insulation and complete the circuit. You do not have to strip the wires.

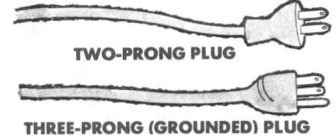

Figure 5-3: Wired plugs may have two or three prongs.

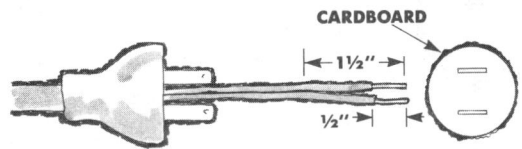

Figure 5-4: With a two prong plug, separate the wires for about an inch and a half and strip off the insulation for about ½ inch. Scrape the wire until it shines and twist the copper ends so they hold together.

14 Home Maintenance and Repair

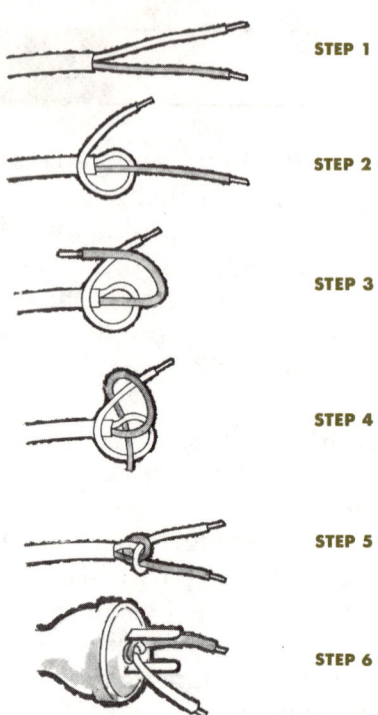

STEP 1
STEP 2
STEP 3
STEP 4
STEP 5
STEP 6

Figure 5-5: Tie an underwriters knot in this way. This knot puts the pull on the insulation instead of the wire. If this knot is not used, the wire may come loose in a short time, especially if the plug is removed by pulling on the cord.

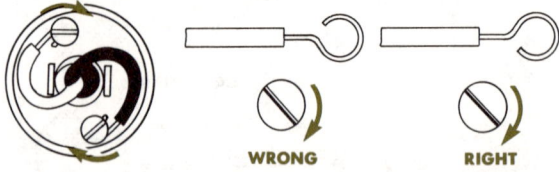

Figure 5-6: After the knot is pulled into the plug cap, the stripped wire is wound around the screws in the direction that the screw will be turned to tighten. This pulls the wire in under the screw. If the wire is looped in the opposite direction it will be pushed away as the screw is tightened.

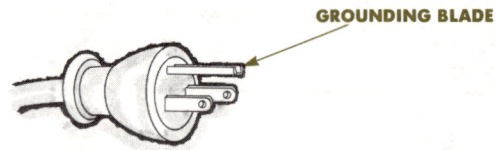

Figure 5-7: A three-prong plug has one prong longer than the two prongs that carry the current. This grounding prong insures a good ground connection.

Figure 5-8: Installing a three-prong plug is similar to installing a two-prong plug. Be sure to connect each wire to the proper terminal. The extra prong is always the ground.

plug. Make an underwriters knot with the black and white wires. Attach the third green wire to the green screw (figure 5-8). Attach the white wire to the silver screw and black wire to the brass screw. Be sure none of the bare wires are touching each other. Replace the protective cover.

Some plugs are completely cased in rubber. If one of these plugs goes bad, unplug the appliance and cut off the bad plug. Then install a new one following one of the methods explained.

SELF CHECK

1. What are some things that may go wrong with a plug?
2. How can you repair a two-prong, wired plug?
3. How do you tie an underwriters knot?
4. Where should you attach each of the wires in a three-prong plug?

CORDS AND SOCKETS — Unit 6

Appliance wire is a good conductor, but it pulls apart easily. The wires inside most electrical cords are in strands (figure 6-1). They are not solid like permanent wiring in the walls. The insulation around the wires is strong and helps hold the strands together. The wire usually breaks before the insulation does (figure 6-2)

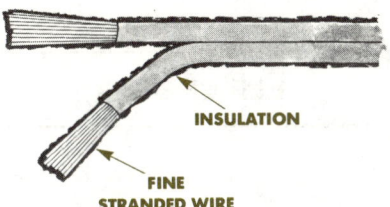

Figure 6-1: So they will be flexible, most lamp and appliance cords are made of hair-like strands of metal in an insulated shell.

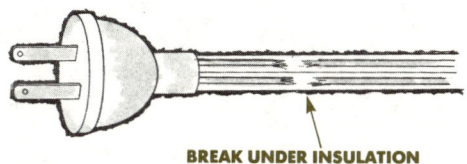

Figure 6-2: A wire may break or burn through under the insulation. Broken wire can cause sparking that will burn the insulation.

and you will not be able to see where it is broken. When the wire breaks, the lamp may go out entirely. If you move the cord or hold it a certain way, the lamp may go on again.

To check a lamp cord, plug it in and use a circuit tester to test the ends of the wire closest to the lamp. If the tester lights, the circuit is complete and there is nothing wrong with the cord. Most likely, the lamp socket is defective. If the circuit tester does not light up, flex the cord and see if this makes the circuit tester flicker. Be very careful while the cord is plugged in.

If the cord is bad, remove it. A replacement cord has a molded plug at one end and bare wires at the other (figure 6-3). Be sure to replace the cord with one exactly the same. Heating

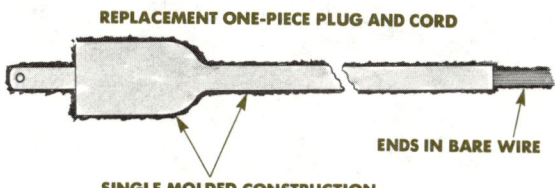

Figure 6-3: Many replacement lamp cords come with a molded plug as part of a one-piece assembly.

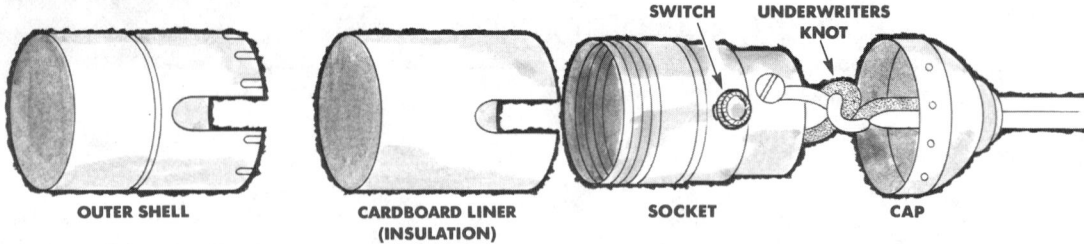

Figure 6-4: There is a spot marked PRESS on the brass outer shell of the lamp. By pressing this spot and wiggling the lamp socket, you can separate the parts. The switch in the socket is usually the defective part. Always replace the cardboard liner.

devices especially require a special type of cord. Attach the new cord exactly as the old cord was attached.

If the cord is good, but the lamp still doesn't light, the problem is usually the lamp socket, which contains the switch. The lamp socket has four basic parts (figure 6-4):

- Cap
- Socket
- Cardboard liner
- Outer shell

When you buy a new socket, be sure to get the same kind. Although they may look alike, sockets come in different sizes and types.

Before working on the lamp socket, unplug the lamp and remove the bulb. On the outer shell there is a spot marked PRESS. By pressing and wiggling it, you can remove the outer shell and the cardboard liner. Unless the cap is damaged it probably does not need to be replaced. In the cap, the wires are tied in an underwriters knot. Examine the wires. If the insulation is brittle, cut back the wires or replace them. Tie an underwriters knot. Then attach the ends of the wires to the new socket just as they were on the old socket. Set the socket back in the cap. Replace the cardboard liner. Plug in the lamp and test it.

SELF CHECK

1. Why may a lamp work despite a broken cord?
2. How do you check a lamp cord?
3. What are four parts of a lamp socket?
4. How should you replace a lamp socket?

| OUTLETS AND SWITCHES | Unit 7 |

Two electrical devices in the home are in constant use. They are:
- Outlet receptacles
- Switches

Both of these devices are housed in electrical boxes (figure 7-1) made of metal or plastic. In the box, the outlet or switch is attached to wires that carry the house current.

Figure 7-2: The electrical box often contains an outlet receptacle. Lamps and appliances can be plugged into these outlet receptacles.

An outlet receptacle includes one or more electrical sockets (figure 7-2) connected to the wires inside the box. A two-prong plug inserted into the outlet connects to two hot wires. This permits electricity to flow through the lamp or appliance.

If a receptacle breaks or wears out, it must be replaced. Test the outlet with

Figure 7-3: A broken or worn out outlet receptacle cannot be repaired. Test for electricity by inserting the two prongs of a circuit tester into the two slots of the outlet. If it lights there is electrical flow. If not, replace the outlet.

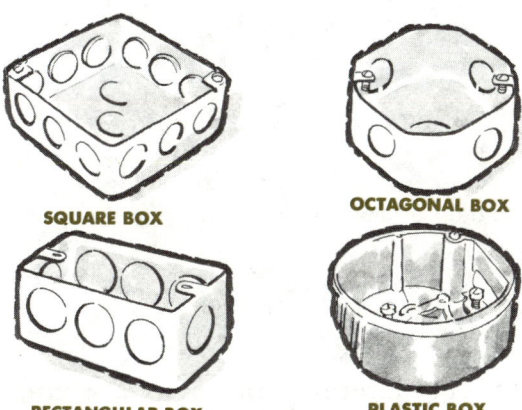

Figure 7-1: Electrical boxes are generally secured to wall studs and hold the wires that attach to outlets and switches. They are usually made of metal. Sometimes boxes are made of bakelite, a type of plastic especially good in damp locations.

a circuit tester (figure 7-3). If it does not light, replace the outlet.

First turn off the electricity by removing the fuse or turning off the circuit breaker. In some cases you may want to turn off all the electricity at the main switch.

17

18 Home Maintenance and Repair

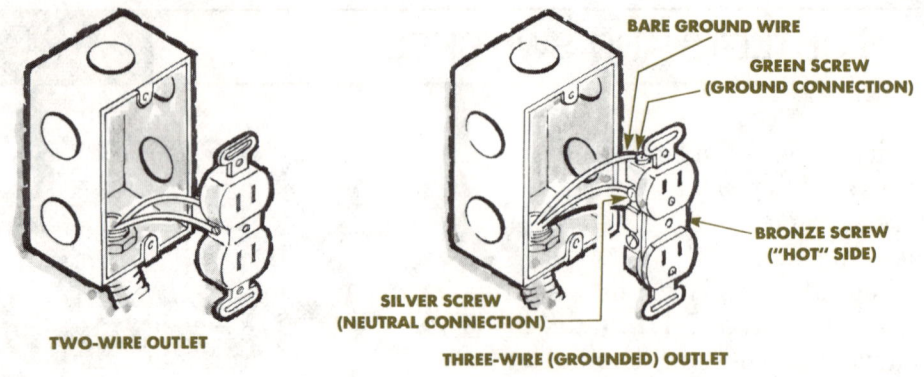

Figure 7-4: Remove the outlet from the box. Many outlets are connected by two wires. Others, the grounded type, have three wires.

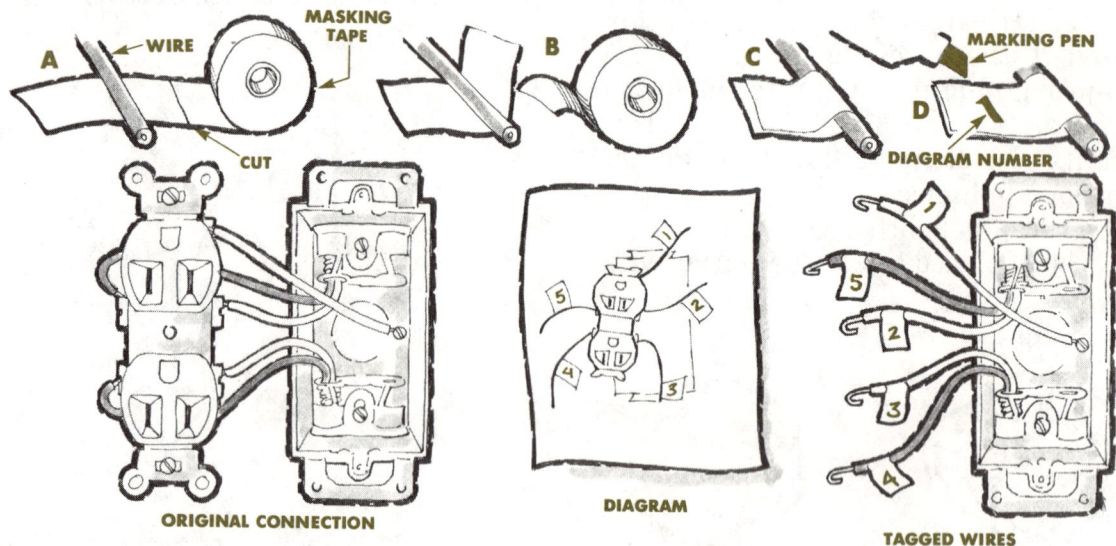

Figure 7-5: Label each wire and diagram the connections before removing the outlet.

Remove the face plate and unscrew the outlet from the box (figure 7-4). Draw a diagram of how each wire is connected to the outlet. Label each wire with a letter or number on masking tape (figure 7-5) before you disconnect the wires. Be sure to mark the letter or number on your diagram. Sometimes receptacles seem to have more wires than they need. This is because the receptacle itself makes the connection and continues the circuit to the next outlet somewhere else in the house (figure 7-6).

Outlets and Switches 19

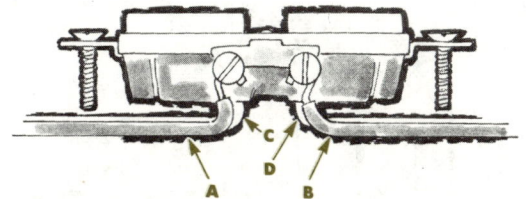

Figure 7-6: Sometimes outlets are wired to one another. Instead of continuing straight through, the line stops at one set of screws on the outlet. Both screws on the same side of the outlet are connected so that the next set of wires carries electricity just as if A was connected directly to B.

Figure 7-8: Outlet receptacles within a room are sometimes turned OFF or ON by a switch.

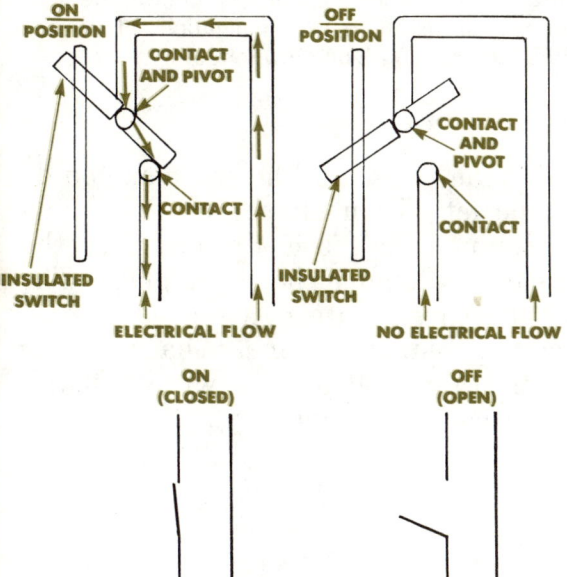

Figure 7-7: Switches open and close the circuit.

Figure 7-9: An electrical box may house a switch and an outlet together.

Attach the new outlet according to your diagram. Be sure all wires are bent properly and screwed down tight. Loose wires cause sparks, and sparks can cause fires.

The outlet receptacle has slotted holes at the top and bottom (figure 7-2).

This is so you can hang the outlet straight even if the box is crooked. When you replace the face plate, no one can see that the box is not straight.

There are many types of switches, but all of them work by opening or closing a circuit (figure 7-7). Electricity will not flow through an open circuit. Switches in outlet housings usually control lights, air conditioners, and other built-in house appliances through in-wall wiring. Sometimes the switch will control outlet receptacles elsewhere in the room (figure 7-8) or in the same housing (figure 7-9).

20 Home Maintenance and Repair

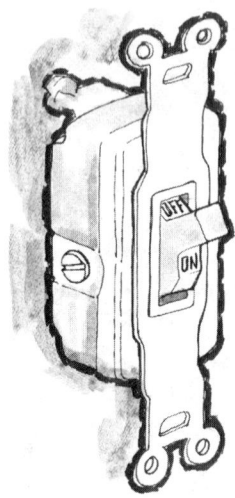

Figure 7-10: A single-pole switch is marked OFF and ON. It controls a circuit from one point.

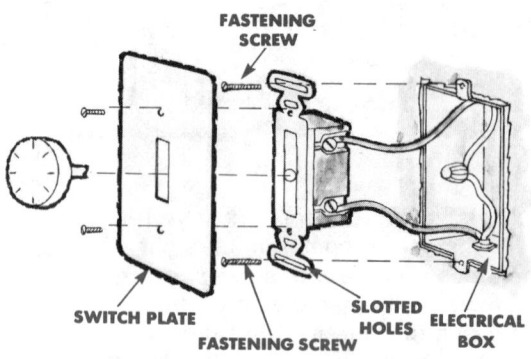

Figure 7-11: Dimmer switches control the light intensity from off to full illumination. They are installed like single-pole switches.

The simplest switch is a single pole single throw switch (figure 7-10). This switch is marked ON and OFF. In the ON or up position, the circuit is closed and electricity flows through the switch. In the OFF or down position, the circuit is opened, stopping the flow of electricity. Do not install a switch upside down.

Two three-way switches are used to control a circuit from two different locations. They are used in hallways and stairways, for example. Three-way switches are not marked ON/OFF.

Other special switches are used for safety. Dimmer switches (figure 7-11) can be used to brighten or dim the lights by turning a knob. Mercury switches, which don't spark, are used where inflammable or explosive materials might be present. They will not work if mounted upside down. Outdoor switches and outlets should be grounded and sealed against moisture.

Replace a switch the same as you do an outlet. Turn off the electricity by removing the fuse or opening the breaker. Remove the cover plate. The switch cover plate is attached by two screws instead of one. Diagram the connections and tag the wires. Install the new switch and replace the cover plate.

SELF CHECK

1. Name two electrical devices that are installed in electrical boxes.
2. What does an outlet receptacle do?
3. How does a switch work?
4. What is the best way to determine how to attach the wires to a new switch or outlet receptacle?

WIRE SPLICES   Unit 8

Most home wiring can be joined with splices. A splice is made by twisting two or more pieces of wire together. All wire splices must be made in an electrical box. The three splices most often used in home repair are:

- Pigtail splice
- Tap splice
- Western Union splice

The pigtail splice (figure 8-1) is a quick and easy way to connect two wires. Twist the ends of the wires together. Then tape the end or attach a solderless connector (figure 8-2). The pigtail splice is weak. Use it only where the wires will not be pulled.

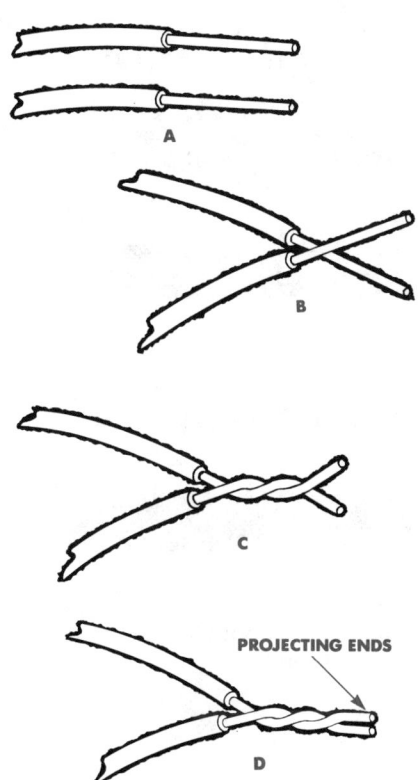

Figure 8-1: The pigtail splice is the quickest and easiest way to connect two wires, but it pulls apart easily.

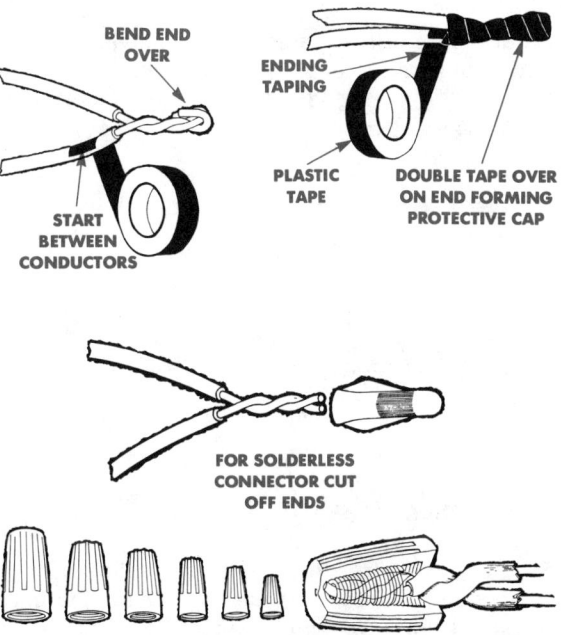

Figure 8-2: In a pigtail splice the ends are taped or joined by solderless connectors.

21

22 Home Maintenance and Repair

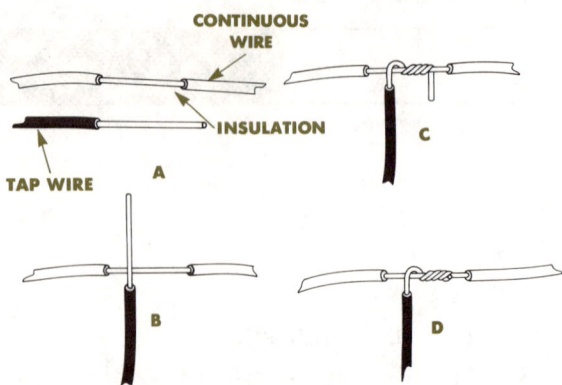

Figure 8-3: In a tap splice the free end of one wire may be connected to the middle of another wire.

Figure 8-4: Be careful when removing insulation. Cut at a 30° angle so you do not nick or cut the wire. A damaged wire will not conduct electricity well and may break.

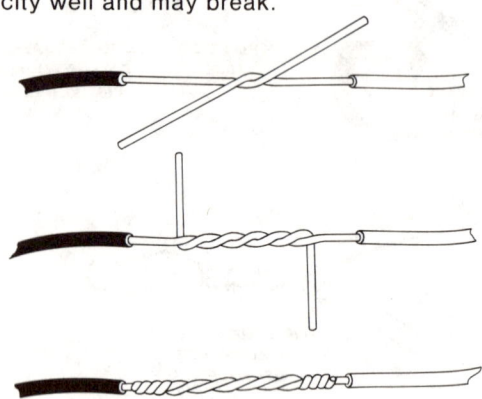

Figure 8-5: The Western Union splice is the strongest. It is used where the connection may be pulled. First twist the wires for 1 to 2 inches at the center. Then tightly wrap one end five or six times around the other wire. Do the same with the other end.

The tap splice (figure 8-3) joins a cut wire to a continuous wire. Remove about an inch of insulation from a midpoint in the continuous wire (figure 8-4). Then wind the tap (cut) wire around the exposed portion of the continuous wire. Insulate the splice with tape.

The Western Union splice (figure 8-5) is the strongest splice. It conducts electricity well and withstands strain. The secret is to wrap the end of each wire around the body of the other wire. Use tape to insulate it (figure 8-6).

A fire from bad wiring usually starts at a splice or outlet connection. When splicing wires, scrape the wires clean and twist them snugly. If you don't,

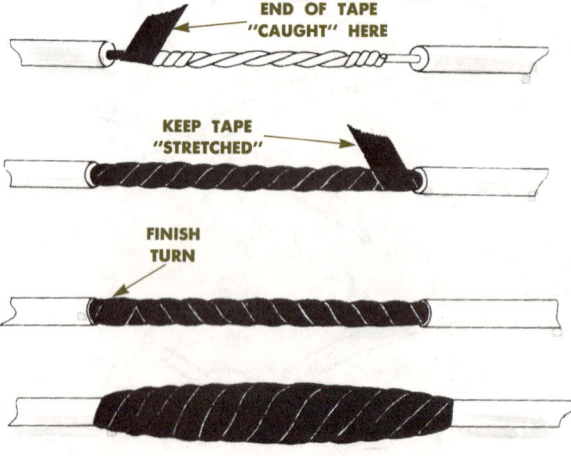

Figure 8-6: Tape a Western Union splice in this way. Keep the tape tight as you wind it around the wire.

Wire Splices

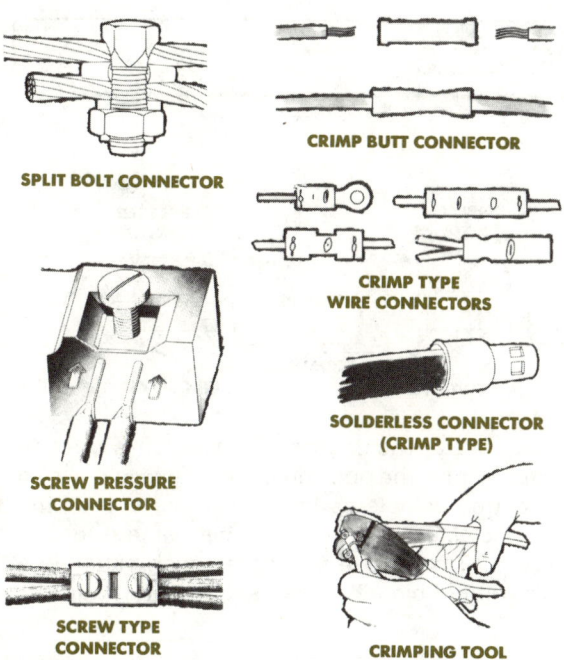

Figure 8-7: Several types of mechanical connectors can be used to join wires.

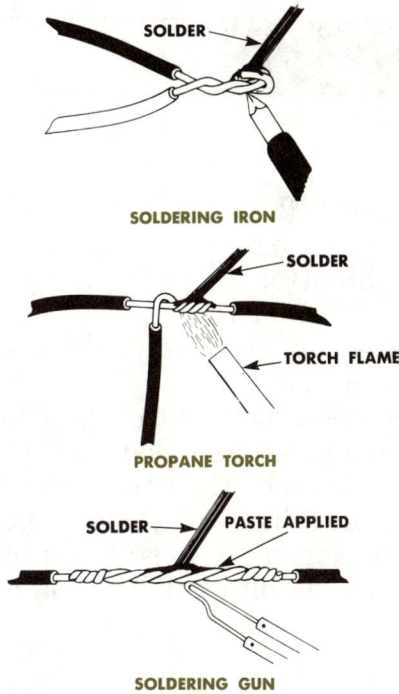

Figure 8-8: Soldered joints. First scrape or sand the wires clean. Apply rosin (not acid) flux at the top. Soldering will make the joint stronger and prevent corrosion.

the splice will get hot. Soon it may arc and you will have a bigger problem to solve than bad wiring—a major fire in your home.

Other methods of joining wires are:
- Mechanical connectors such as electrical clamps (figure 8-7)
- Soldering (figure 8-8)

These methods are not used in most home repairs. However, soldering strengthens the joint and helps prevent corrosion.

SELF CHECK

1. What are the three most common wire splices used in home repair?
2. What is the best way to remove insulation from a wire?
3. How do you make a Western Union splice?
4. What must be done to prevent hot splices?

Unit 9 — DOORBELLS

The doorbell system (figure 9-1) has four working parts:
- Push button
- Transformer
- Electromagnet and striker
- Bell or chime

A doorbell push button is simply a switch with a spring inside (figure 9-2). Pressing down on the button completes the circuit. When you release the button, the spring pushes the contacts open and cuts off electrical flow.

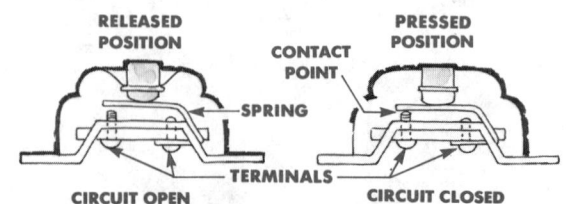

Figure 9-2: The doorbell push button is a spring switch kept in the open position. Pushing down on the button completes the circuit and sounds the bell or chime. Doorbell push buttons are for low voltage. Do not use a doorbell push button in a high voltage circuit. It can arc and start a fire.

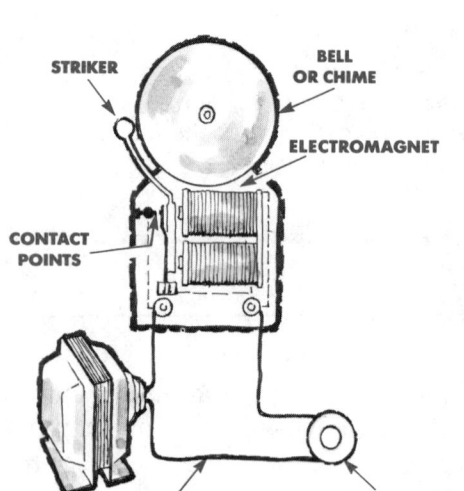

Figure 9-1: Doorbells and chimes have the same basic working parts. A bell, though, also has a set of contact points that are pulled apart each time the electromagnet draws the striker. This opens the circuit. A spring pulls the contacts together again and the cycle repeats as long as the pushbutton is held. This is why doorbells keep ringing and chimes only sound once.

Figure 9-3: The input side of a transformer is connected to the 110-volt house current. The two contacts on the output side give 8 to 20 volts to operate the doorbell.

A transformer is a device that changes voltage. There are two basic types of transformers:
- A step-up transformer, which increases voltage
- A step-down transformer, which cuts down voltage

A doorbell transformer (figure 9-3) is the step-down type. It takes 110-volt current and reduces it to a low voltage of 8 to 20 volts. This low voltage output operates the doorbell. Eight to 20 volts is relatively safe. The high voltage wired into the other side of the transformer is dangerous.

When you push the doorbell button, electricity flows through an electromagnet which attracts a striker. As the striker moves, it hits the bell (figure 9-4) or chime (figure 9-5).

If the doorbell is not working, first inspect the wiring. Splice any broken wire or replace it with No. 18 bell wire.

Probably the most common problem with doorbells is the push button because it must stand up under constant use and weather conditions. To check it, remove the mounting screws and inspect the back. Clamp a piece of wire with alligator clips across the contacts (figure 9-6). If you don't have alligator clips, hold a piece of wire by the insulation and touch the bare ends of the wire to the contacts. If the doorbell rings, the push button is faulty. First try cleaning the contacts with steel

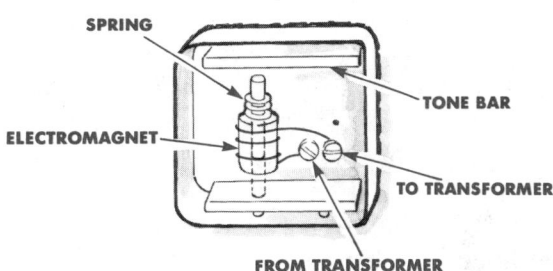

Figure 9-5: A chime unit is similar to a doorbell without contact points. The electromagnet pulls a soft iron plunger into the coil. The plunger strikes the bottom tone bar. A spring pulls the plunger back up and the plunger then strikes the top tone bar.

Figure 9-4: The operation of the doorbell depends on electrical current flowing through an electromagnet. The magnet attracts the striker, which in turn strikes the bell.

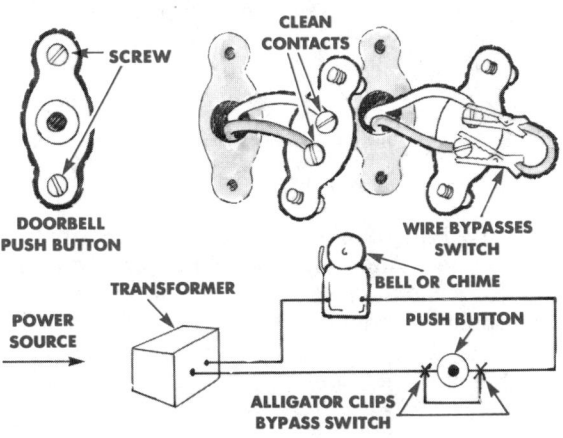

Figure 9-6: Because the push button has a spring and is exposed to the weather, it is usually one of the first things that fails. A way to check it is to remove the doorbell and close the circuit with a piece of wire. If the closed doorbell circuit rings, the problem is the push button. If the bell doesn't ring, the problem is somewhere else.

wool or fine sandpaper. If that doesn't work, replace the push button.

When you bypass the switch and the doorbell still does not ring, the problem is somewhere else in the circuit. Next test the transformer at the low voltage side. This is the side connected to the wires that run to the push button and the bell, figure 9-3. Test it with a low voltage circuit tester. A 110-volt tester will not work. If the circuit tester lights, the transformer is working and the problem is with the doorbell or chime itself. If the tester does not light the transformer is bad and must be replaced with one of the same voltage. Turn off the electricity. Loosen and remove the locknut behind the transformer (figure 9-7). Replace the transformer with a new one having the same voltage. Remove the wires and attach the new transformer in the same way the old one was attached.

If the doorbell or chime itself is the problem, you may be able to fix it. Check the wires connected to the bell or chime unit to make sure they haven't come loose. You may have to bend the striker slightly so that it will make contact with the bell. If the chime unit has a plunger, cleaning the plunger may help it move more freely. Do not oil the plunger because oil will attract dust, and before long the plunger will be sticking again. Lubricate with silicone spray or graphite. If you cannot repair the chime or bell, it is easy and economical to replace it.

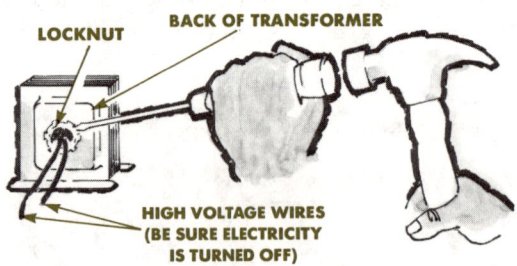

Figure 9-7: There is a locknut at the back of the transformer. After you have turned off the electricity, loosen the locknut by tapping with a hammer and screwdriver. Then unthread the locknut by hand. Be sure the replacement transformer has the same voltage.

SELF CHECK

1. How does a doorbell push button work?
2. What is the difference between the low voltage side and the high voltage side of a transformer?
3. How does a door chime work?
4. What are some things that may go wrong with a doorbell or chime unit?

FLUORESCENT LIGHTS — Unit 10

Fluorescent lights use less electricity and give off less heat than regular lights. They also last much longer and provide more light. Fluorescent light fixtures now being used include two basic types:
- Starter-type fluorescent tube
- Rapid-start fluorescent tube

The starter-type fluorescent fixture (figure 10-1) has a fixture ballast, starter, and the tube itself. Rapid-start fluorescent fixtures do not have a starter (figure 10-2).

If a fluorescent light goes out, check the house fuse or circuit breaker first. If a light blinks on and off, remove the

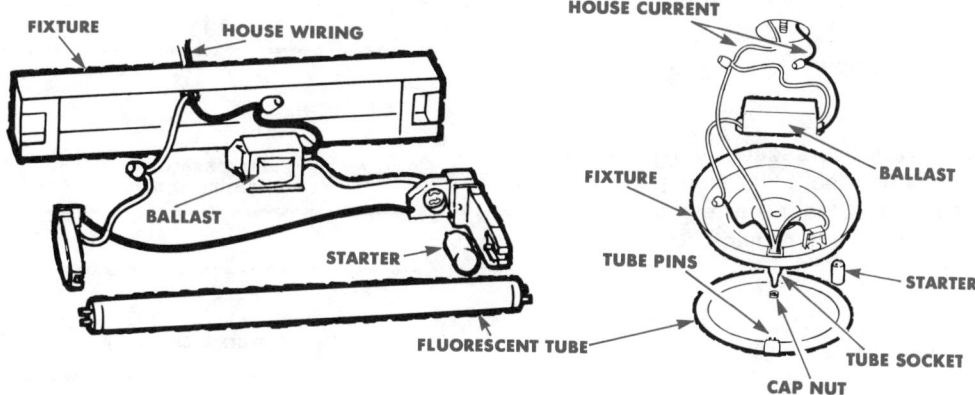

Figure 10-1: The main parts of a starter-type fluorescent tube are the fixture, ballast, starter, and tube. The starter, in connection with the ballast, starts an arc within the tube and causes the inside coating to give off light.

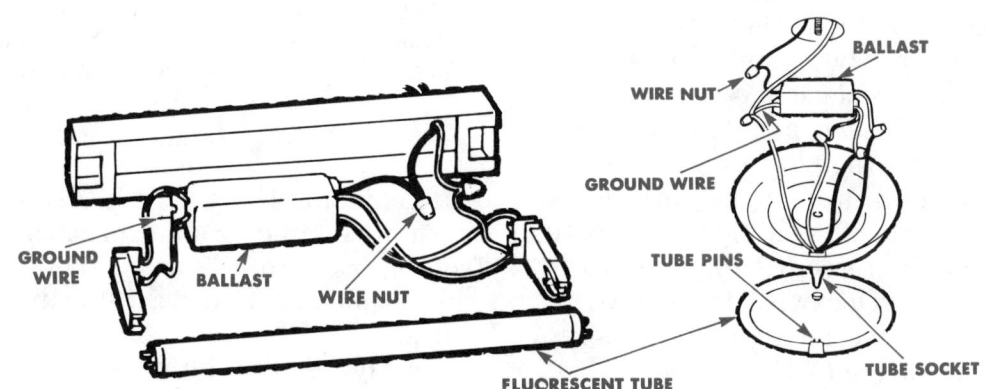

Figure 10-2: There is no starter in a rapid-start fluorescent tube. The ballast alone starts the current.

28 Home Maintenance and Repair

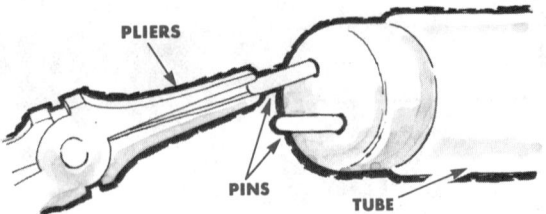

Figure 10-3: Pins in the end of a fluorescent tube may get bent. Straighten them with needle-nose pliers.

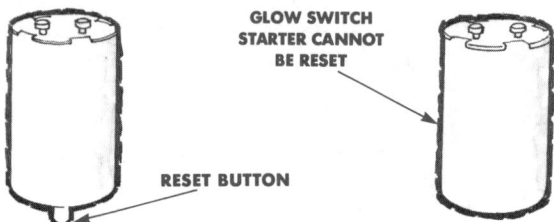

Figure 10-4: If the fluorescent light goes out, sometimes it may be reset by pressing the reset button in the starter. Most starters cannot be reset, but they are easy to replace.

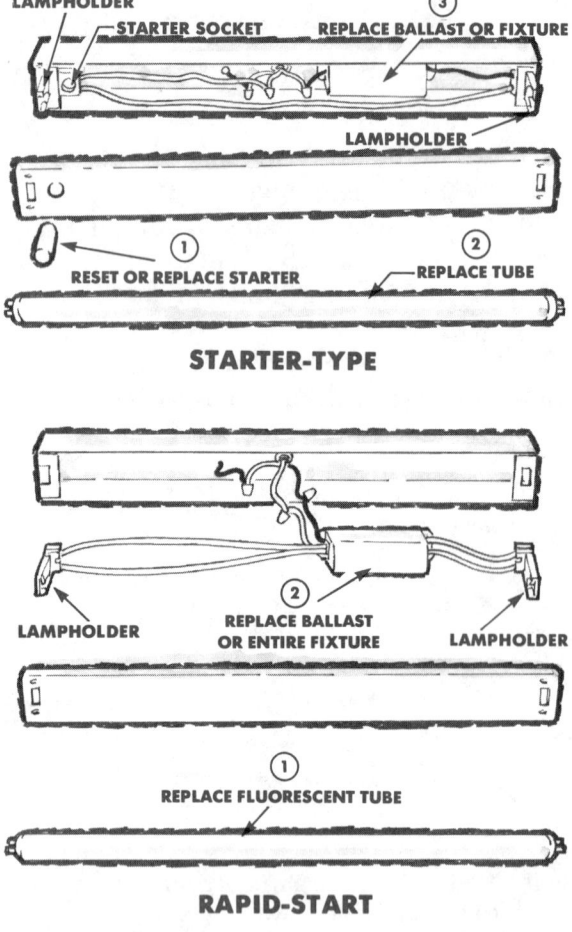

Figure 10-5: To repair a starter-type fluorescent tube, first reset or replace the starter, then the tube, and finally the ballast. For a rapid-start tube, begin with the tube, then the ballast.

tube and check that the pins on the ends are straight and clean. Straighten the pins with needle-nose pliers (figure 10-3). Clean the pins with sandpaper and brush them clean.

In a starter-type system, it is most economical to replace the starter first. Some starters have a button to reset them manually (figure 10-4). However, the most common type must be replaced. Turn off the electricity and remove the fluorescent tube. Turn the starter counterclockwise to remove it. Be sure the replacement starter has the same watts rating as the old one. Most new model fixtures do not use starters anymore.

If replacing the starter doesn't work, try a new tube. Sometimes the light from a new tube swirls and flickers. This is normal and will stop in a few hours.

Finally, if the light still does not work, replace the ballast—the most expensive part (figure 10-5). Insulation

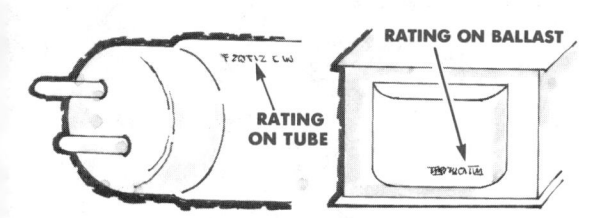

Figure 10-6: Tubes, starters, and ballasts must all have the same rating when used in the same fixture. The rating is the number of watts.

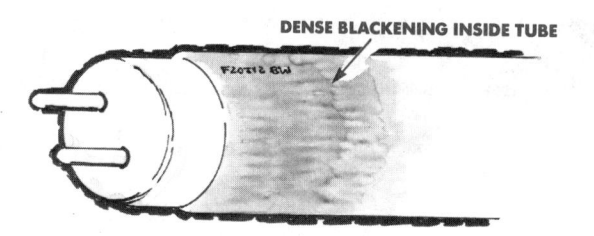

Figure 10-7: It is normal for the ends of a tube to turn brown or gray. When the color is dense black, the tube or the starter should be replaced.

tar leaking along the ballast indicates a faulty ballast. Be sure the ballast has the same rating as the old one (figure 10-6). Replace the ballast carefully, one connection at a time. You may decide to replace the entire fixture for a little more than the cost of the ballast.

Noisy fixtures may have loose connections. A special low-noise ballast is also available to make the fixture quieter. Discoloration at the ends of the tubes is normal (figure 10-7). If the ends of an old tube are very dark, the tube is worn out. A new tube that turns black indicates a bad starter.

Most fluorescent lights won't work at temperatures below 50°F. If you need one for a cold area, such as a garage, you can buy a special cold-temperature fixture.

Screw-in types of fluorescent fixtures are also available. The entire fixture is screwed into a regular threaded light socket.

SELF CHECK

1. What are some advantages of fluorescent lights?
2. In what order should you replace the parts of a fluorescent light?
3. How is a starter replaced?
4. What does it mean when the ends of a fluorescent tube are black?

Unit 11   METER READING

Every house has an electrical meter (figure 11-1). The meter keeps track of the electricity used. By reading the meter regularly and keeping records, you can get a good idea of when and where you are using the most electricity. For instance, when the air conditioner is on, you will use a lot more electricity than when it isn't. Leaving a color television on for a long time will make a big difference too. The electric company reads this meter to determine your electric bill.

You will notice that some of the dials on the meter read counterclockwise. To read the meter, start from the left. The dial hand is usually between two numbers, (figure 11-2). Write down the smaller number. Continue reading each dial the same way. Remember the numbers on the second and fourth dials run counterclockwise. The final number completes your reading and tells you how many kilowatt-hours you have used. A kilowatt-hour

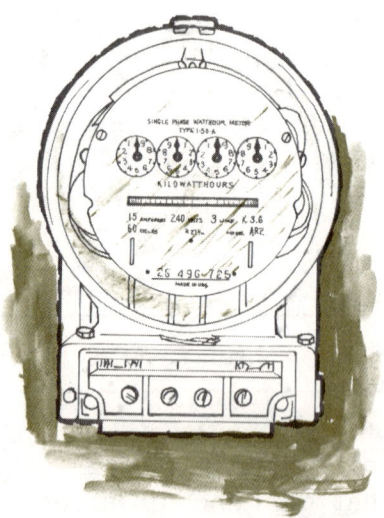

Figure 11-1: The hands on the dial faces turn the same direction as the gears under the dials. So every other dial is numbered backwards or counterclockwise.

Figure 11-2: Each dial hand is usually between two numbers. To read the meter just read the lowest of the two numbers on all dials.

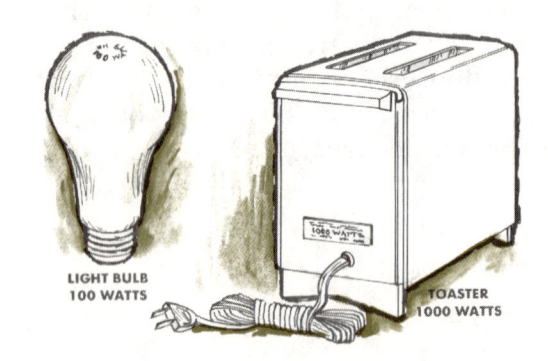

Figure 11-3: A 100-watt light bulb will take 10 hours to burn 1000 watts (one kilowatt). A thousand-watt toaster burns one kilowatt (1 kw) in one hour.

30

Figure 11-4: Electric meters can be read daily. The difference between the two readings is the amount of electricity used that day.

(abbreviated kwh) is one kilowatt of electricity (one thousand watts) being used for one hour (figure 11-3).

If you read the meter the next day and subtract the first day's reading, you will know the total number of kilowatt-hours used during that day (figure 11-4).

Now you can calculate your bill for any period of time. If, for example, you wanted to figure your bill for the month of March, you would take a reading on the first day of March and again on the first day of April. Subtract to figure out how many kilowatt-hours were used:

Reading on April 1: 2403
Reading on March 1: 1635
768 kwh used during March.

Multiply this by the rate shown on your bill and add other charges to calculate your month's bill:

Rate 768 x $0.0433 = $33.25
Fuel Adjustment 768 x $0.00612 = 4.70
(changes each month)
37.95
Add taxes

SELF CHECK

1. What is the purpose of an electrical meter?
2. If the dial hand on an electrical meter falls between two numbers, which one do you read?
3. What is a kilowatt-hour?
4. Check your electrical meter for three days at the same time of day to determine on which day you used the most electricity.

3 PLUMBING

No one wants to live without good plumbing. Hot and cold running water, toilets that flush, and drains that drain are as much a part of modern living as electricity. Good plumbing is more than a convenience. It is a necessity that has done more to prevent disease than any other civilized invention.

Keeping plumbing in good working condition is a hard and often dirty job. As a consequence, plumbers are well paid. You can save a lot of money by learning to make some of the simpler repairs yourself.

PLUMBING SAFETY — Unit 12

Any plumbing system is based on common sense. In its simplest form, plumbing brings clean water into a home and carries dirty water out. In practice, plumbing systems are a lot more complicated. Working on plumbing requires special care.

If plumbing itself is based on common sense, so is plumbing safety.

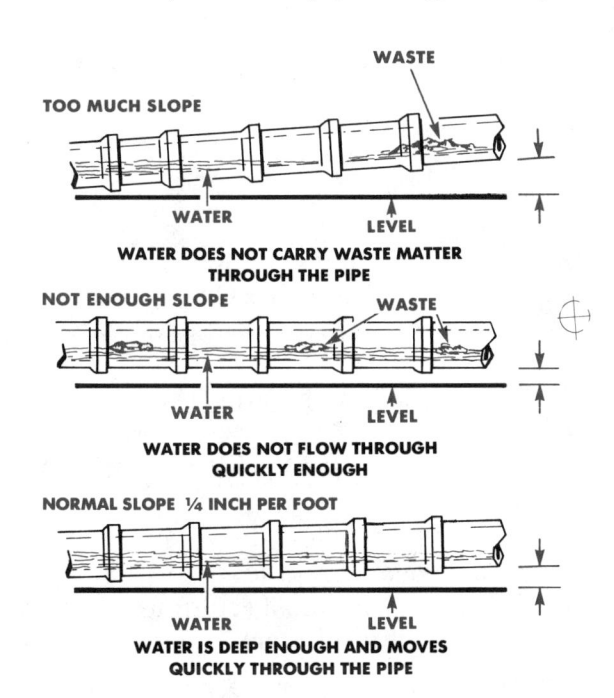

Figure 12-1: Building codes regulate the proper angle for waste water pipes: If a waste pipe slopes too much or too little, the pipe will plug up. This kind of rule protects the person who uses the plumbing.

Every professional or do-it-yourself plumber must think about two groups of people:
- Those who use the plumbing
- Those who work on the plumbing

Building codes are government regulations designed to prevent contamination and disease. Plumbing codes, for example, regulate pipe sizes and the slope of horizontal pipes (figure 12-1). Follow the codes and you will be sure that the plumbing is safe for those who use it.

A plumber's personal safety is important too. When working on any plumbing system the plumber should:
- First turn off the water pressure (figure 12-2)
- Drain hot water pipes before working on them
- Ground all electrical tools. Avoid using electrical equipment in wet areas
- Use the right tool for the job and use it properly (figure 12-3). When wrenches slip off the work, knuckles and hands become bruised. This is the most common plumbing-related injury
- Handle sharp pipes carefully. Pipes that have rusted through are very sharp and can cut easily
- Be sure the system is closed before turning the water on again

34 Home Maintenance and Repair

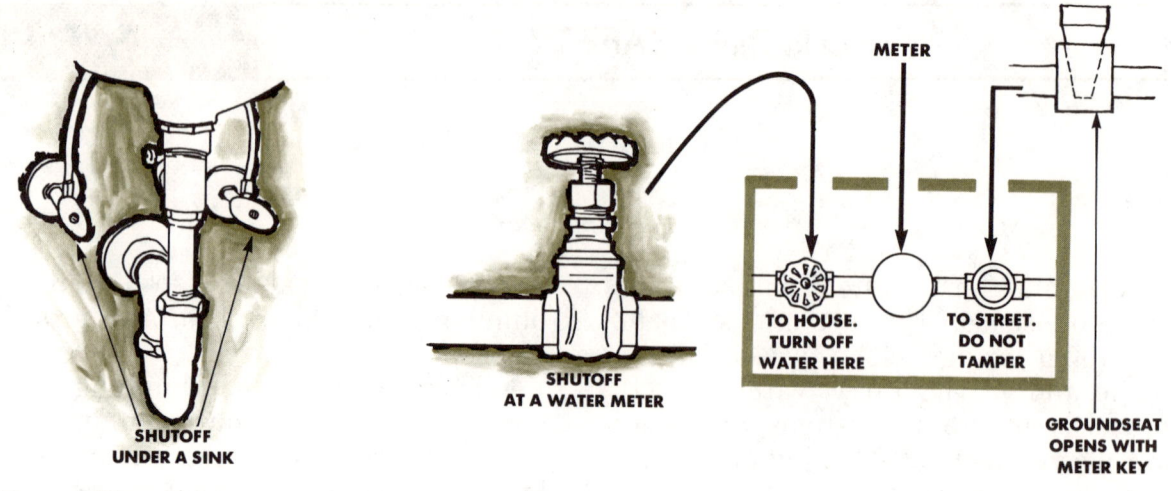

Figure 12-2: Always turn off the water before working on the plumbing system. Water may be turned off at the fixture or at the meter.

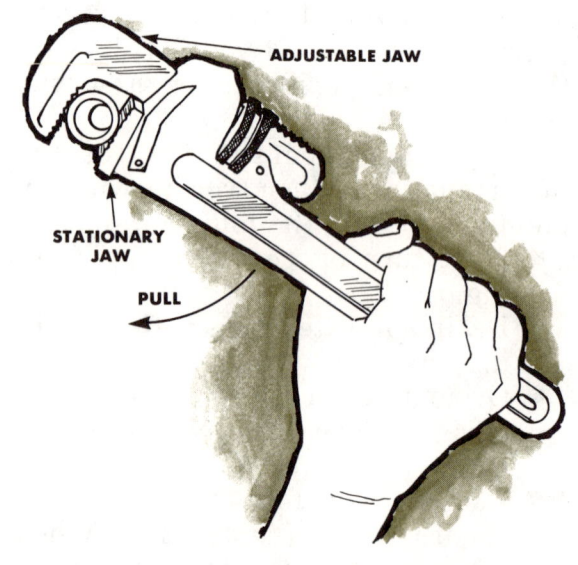

Figure 12-3: Wrenches should fit snugly around the pipe. With adjustable wrenches, the jaws should face the direction of pull.

SELF CHECK

1. Whose safety should the plumber have in mind?
2. What is the purpose for building codes?
3. What should you do when working on a hot water pipe?
4. What is the most common injury from plumbing work?

FAUCETS

Unit 13

The most common household plumbing problem is a dripping faucet. It is annoying and wastes water as well. The cure for a dripping faucet depends on the type of faucet used:
- A compression faucet
- A no-washer faucet

A compression faucet (figure 13-1) presses a washer against a seat by means of a screw thread on the valve stem. This stops water from flowing through the faucet. If the valve seat is corroded or the washer is damaged, water will seep past the valve causing a drip. If the packing is worn, water will leak out around the handle when the faucet is opened.

To repair a compression faucet, turn off the water. Bathroom and kitchen sinks usually have two valves under the sink. They control the hot and cold water. Because they are not used often, these valves may stick. Squirt penetrating oil on the valve stems and wait at least ten minutes. Then try turning the handle back and forth. If it still doesn't move, shut off the water at the meter, and replace the undersink valves before you proceed.

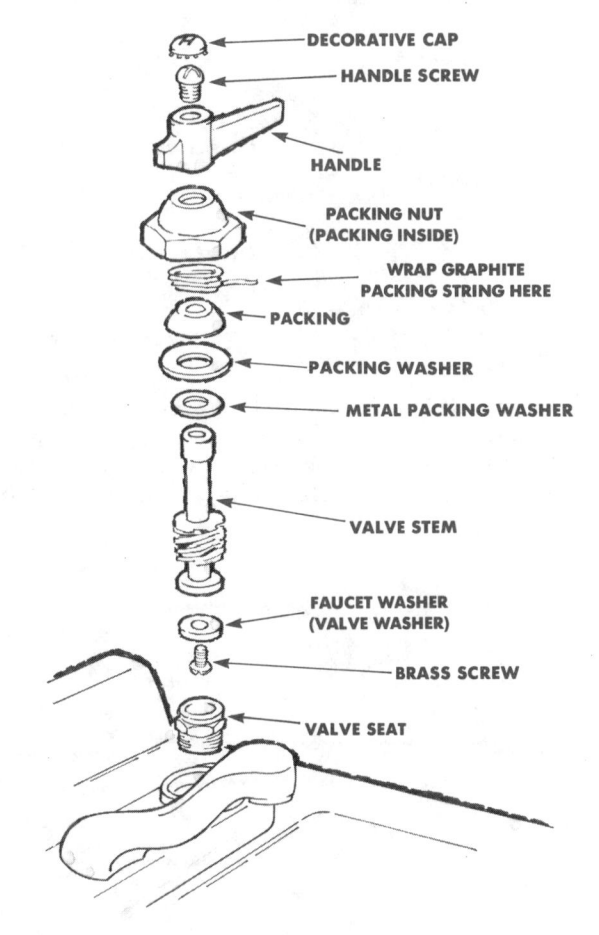

Figure 13-1: Compression faucets work by compressing a washer over the water outlet.

Open the faucet and let the water in the pipes run out. Pipes will drain faster if you can open another faucet higher up to let air in. When the pipes are drained, close the stopper in the sink to avoid dropping any small items down the drain.

If the handle screw is covered with a decorative cap, unscrew or pry the cap off (figure 13-2). Remove the screw and handle.

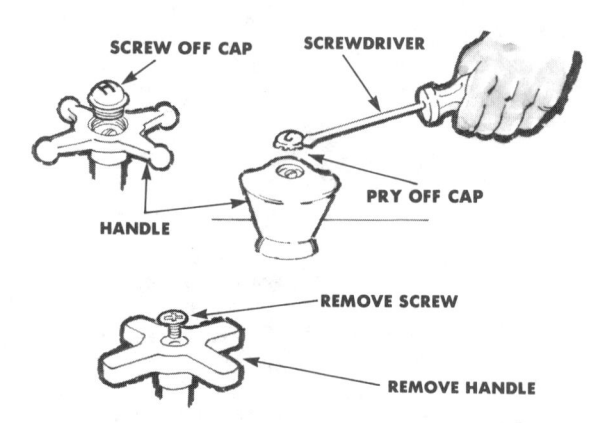

Figure 13-2: To remove the faucet handle, first unscrew or pry up the decorative cap. Remove the handle screw. Then pull up while gently rocking the faucet handle. Use penetrating oil if necessary.

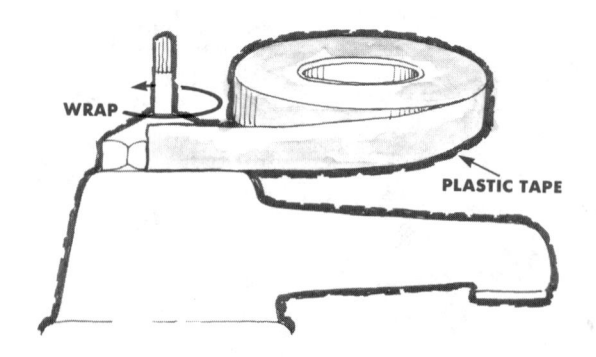

Figure 13-3: To protect the chrome, wind tape around the packing nut before using a wrench.

Wind plastic tape (figure 13-3) or a rag around the packing nut. Remove the nut with an adjustable wrench.

If the faucet has been leaking around the handle, pry out the packing washer and the packing. Wind some packing

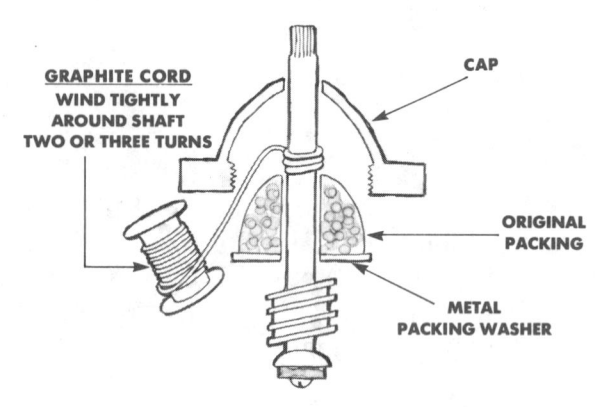

Figure 13-4: Repair worn packing by winding some graphite cord around the valve shaft just above the old packing. Push it up into the cap. You may have to turn the handle a few times after assembly in order to get it to seal properly.

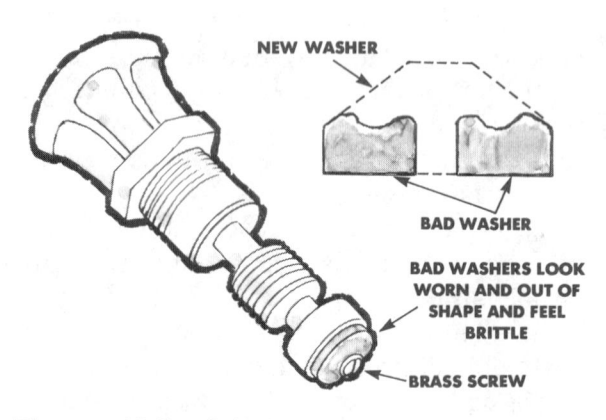

Figure 13-5: Dripping faucets are usually caused by bad washers. Use a soft rubber washer for cold water and a hard rubber or fiber washer for hot water. Washers should not be forced into the stem. If the screw is bad, replace it with a new brass screw. Do not use a steel screw because it will rust.

cord around the shaft above the old packing (figure 13-4). Push up the cord and replace the packing washer. If necessary, use a new washer.

For other leaks, replace the faucet washer (figure 13-5). If the screw is worn or corroded, replace it with a new brass one. Feel the valve seat. If it feels rough or cracked, smooth it with a reaming tool (figure 13-6). Carefully remove only enough metal to smooth the seat. It may be easier and less expensive to replace the entire seat.

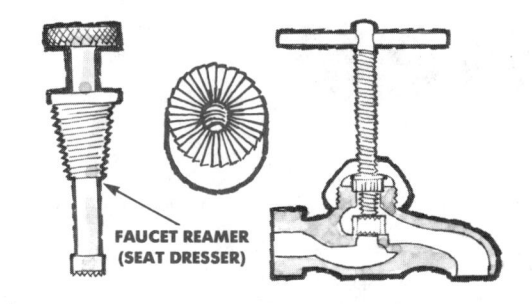

Figure 13-6: A faucet reamer, also called a seat dresser or reseating tool, smoothes the metal seat. Rough valve seats tear up rubber washers. The seat is a soft metal, so remove as little as possible with the reamer.

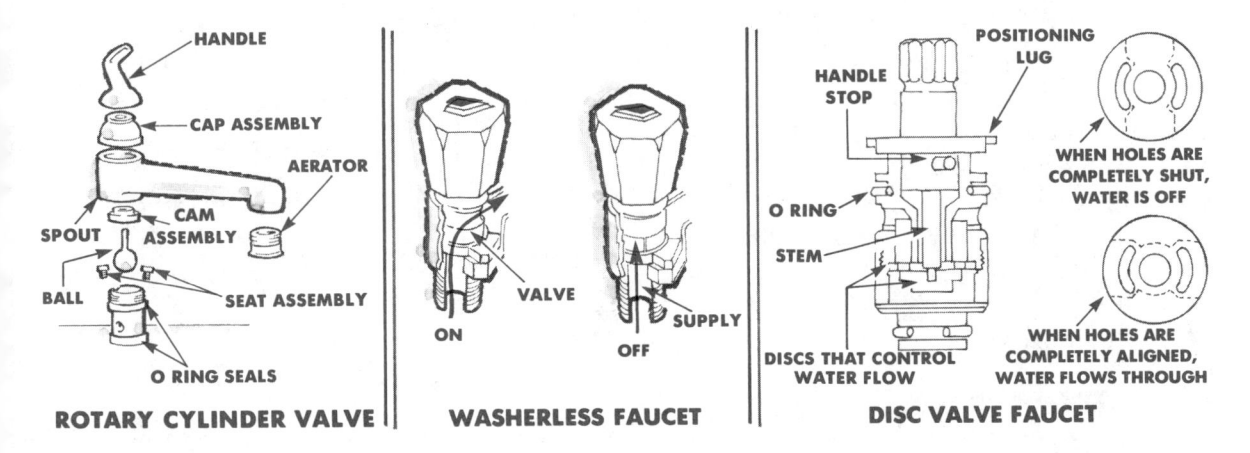

Figure 13-7: There are many washerless faucets. Most do not have packing nuts. None have washers. Water flow is increased or decreased by a hollow sphere or adjustable metal discs similar to air vents.

Washerless faucets do not need to be repaired as often as those with washers. Most of them work by aligning holes to allow the water to flow through (figure 13-7). If repairs are needed you will probably have to replace a major portion with a part that matches exactly. It may be easier, in that case, to replace the entire faucet.

SELF CHECK

1. What are the two main kinds of faucets?
2. What is the most common faucet problem?
3. How do you fix a faucet that leaks around the handle?
4. How do you fix a dripping faucet?

Unit 14 TOILETS

The flush toilet is the most important item in the plumbing system. Sanitation codes require most homes to have one. A non-working toilet is a health hazard.

Toilets are subject to three common problems:
- Wear
- Corrosion
- Clogging

The flush toilet has two major parts, a flush tank and a bowl (figure 14-1). Moving parts in the flush tank (figure 14-2) are the first to wear out or corrode. Clogging usually occurs in the bowl (figure 14-3).

Basically the toilet works because of two valves:
- A float valve
- A flush valve

The float valve is an intake valve that lets water into the tank (figure 14-4). When the tank is full, it automatically shuts off the water. The flush valve

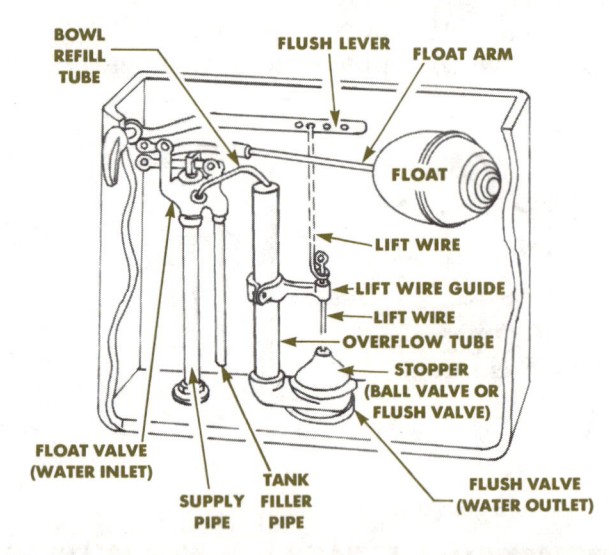

Figure 14-2: The moving parts in a toilet are in the flush tank. This is where most toilet problems occur.

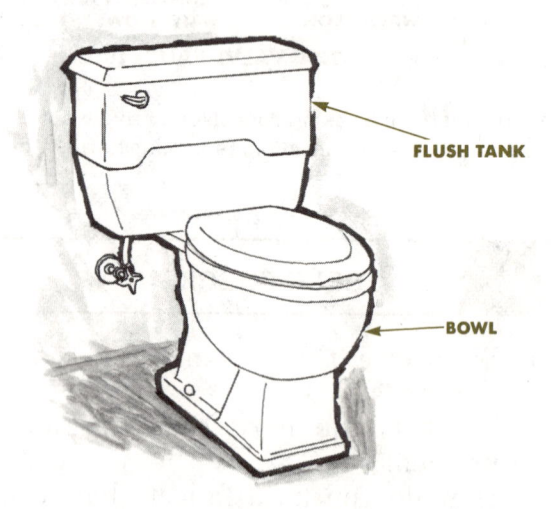

Figure 14-1: Most flush toilets have two major pieces, the flush tank and the bowl.

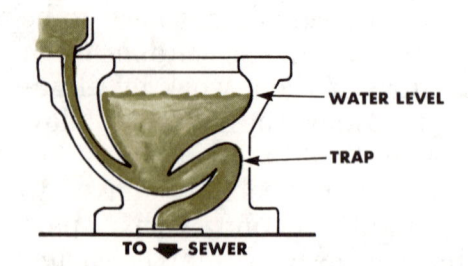

Figure 14-3: The toilet bowl is much simpler. It has a trap similar to the trap under a sink.

Toilets 39

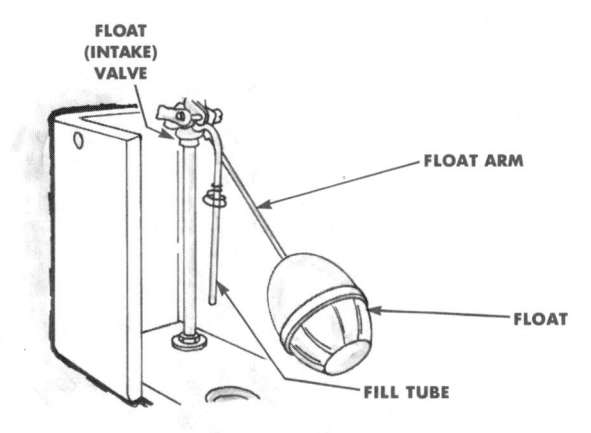

Figure 14-4: The water comes into the toilet tank through the float valve. The rise and fall of the float ball opens and closes the water intake valve. The most common toilet leak occurs when the float arm is out of adjustment. This causes the tank to overfill and water to leak out of the overflow tube.

(figure 14-5), a flapper or ball, lets the water rush out fast enough to keep the bowl clean.

In the flush tank, the water level is controlled by a float arm and ball. The ball is hollow and floats on the water in the tank. When it rises high enough, the float arm closes the inlet valve.

Noise in the tank, no matter how low, is usually a good indication that there is a small leak. If the water keeps running, there is probably an internal leak in the flush tank. No water gets on the floor because it runs down the overflow tube. This often means the float ball is out of adjustment. The first thing to do is raise the ball by hand (figure 14-6). If the water stops, try setting the

Figure 14-5: Water runs from the tank through the flush valve and then through the bowl. The valve must fit snugly into the valve seat. Water will leak out of the flush valve if the seat is in bad condition or the guides are not seating the valve properly.

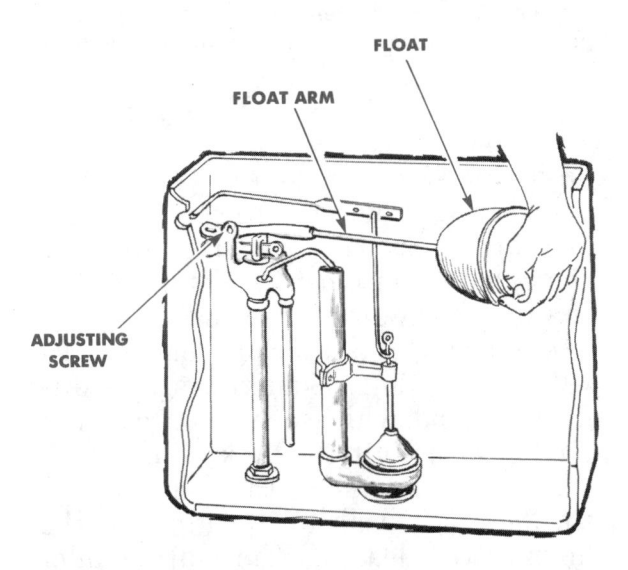

Figure 14-6: Raising the float by hand is a test to see if the intake valve will shut off. If it will, the float needs adjusting. The float arm is adjusted with the adjusting screw at the end of the arm. Sometimes the float arm must also be bent slightly to make the valve close at the proper water level.

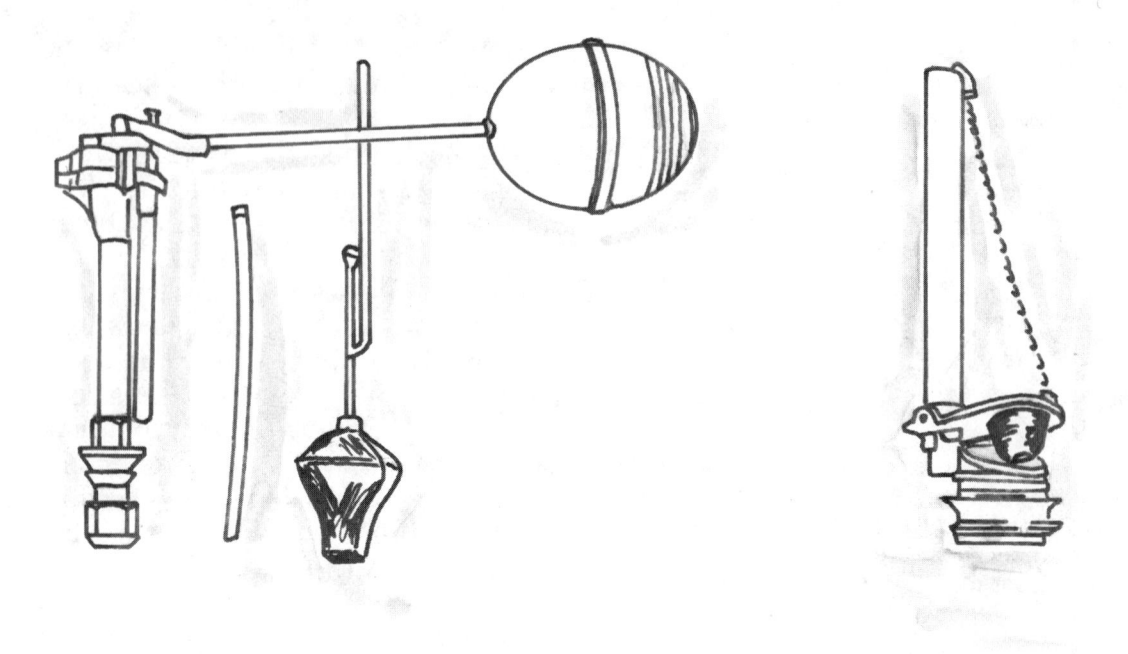

Figure 14-7: Toilet tank repair kits include replacements for flush tank parts. It may be easier to purchase the entire kit than to search for individual parts.

adjusting screw in the end of the float arm. If that doesn't work, bend the float arm. Lowering the float will cause the valve to close before water reaches the top of the overflow tube.

If the water still runs, one of the valves is leaking. Sometimes it is difficult to find which one. You can put food coloring into the tank. Don't flush the toilet. If some of the color gets to the bowl after about 15 minutes, the flush valve is leaking. Turn off the inlet valve under the tank. Feel around the flush valve and the valve seat. Clean it if necessary. Check to see if the valve drops back straight into the center of the valve seat. If not, adjust the lift wire so it does.

When the flush valve does not leak but the tank keeps running down the overflow tube, the problem is probably the float valve. To repair it, turn off the valve below the tank. Take apart the float valve carefully, keeping the parts in order. You may be able to find replacement parts for any that are broken or worn. Most likely you'll have to purchase a toilet tank repair kit (figure 14-7). Most of these kits have plastic fittings. Directions are included.

Sometimes the flush tank will leak water onto the floor. This happens when one of the tank fittings corrodes. Find out where the water is coming from and turn off the inlet valve. Then

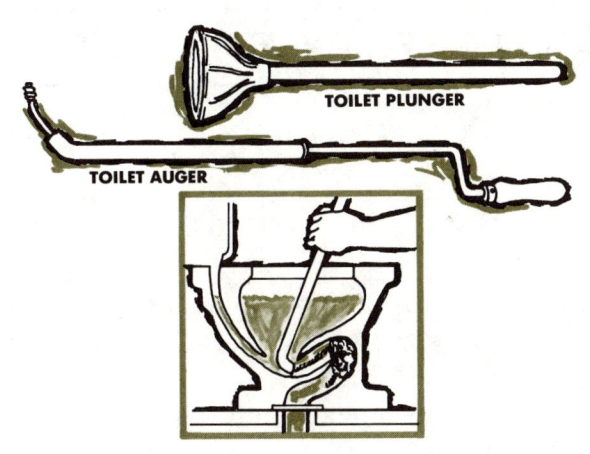

Figure 14-8: A special toilet auger and/or a plunger will fix most toilet clogs.

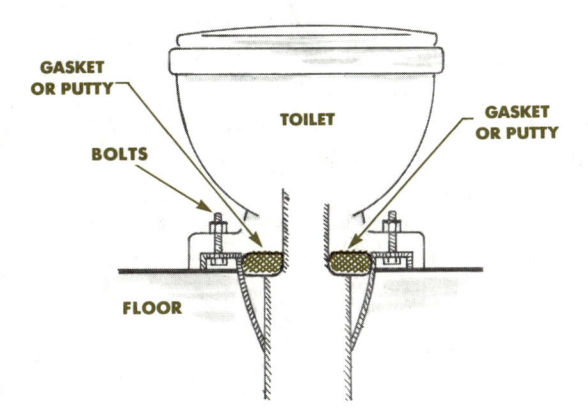

Figure 14-9: If all else fails to unclog a toilet, you will have to drain it, unbolt it, and remove the obstruction. When you replace it, be sure there is a good seal between the bowl and the soil pipe. Be careful not to tighten the bolts too much.

drain the tank by flushing. Remove the fitting and replace the washers. Be careful when replacing the fitting. Turning too tight will crack the flush tank.

Don't be too hasty to replace valves. In a warm, humid house the cold water supply may cause the tank to sweat rather than leak. You can get a special fitting that lets a little hot water into the tank with each flush.

Toilet bowls seldom plug up unless something that doesn't belong there has been dropped in. Often a wire hanger or a plunger will remove it. You may need to use a special toilet auger (figure 14-8). As a last resort only, it may be necessary to shut off the water, drain the tank, and take up the bowl to reach the obstruction from below (figure 14-9). Use a new gasket between the toilet and soil pipe. Be careful when tightening the bolts so that you don't crack the toilet bowl.

SELF CHECK

1. What are the three causes of toilet problems?
2. What happens when the float ball is raised?
3. How can you tell if a flush valve is leaking?
4. How do you unclog the toilet bowl?

Unit 15 PIPES AND PIPE FITTINGS

Five different kinds of pipe are used in most homes:
- Black iron pipe
- Galvanized pipe
- Copper tubing
- Plastic pipe
- Clay sewer pipe

Iron and steel pipes are threaded and may be screwed together. Pipe joint compound or teflon tape on the male threads will help prevent leaks and make it easy to join the pipe and fittings together. Be careful not to break the pipes by screwing them together too tightly.

Black iron pipes should be used only for gas lines.

Galvanizing is a coating of zinc that slows down the rusting of pipes. After several years, the pipe will rust. So, whenever possible, use copper tubing to replace galvanized pipe. Copper costs more, but it doesn't rust, lasts longer, does not need to be threaded, and can be bent around obstacles. Copper also weighs less and is easier to install.

However, where copper touches galvanized pipe, the copper will begin

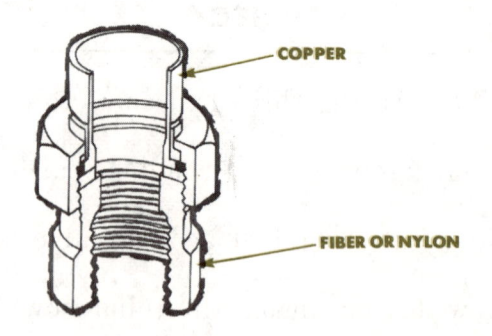

Figure 15-1: An insulated union is used to join copper and iron pipe. It prevents electrolysis by keeping the pipes from touching. The insulator is usually fiber or nylon.

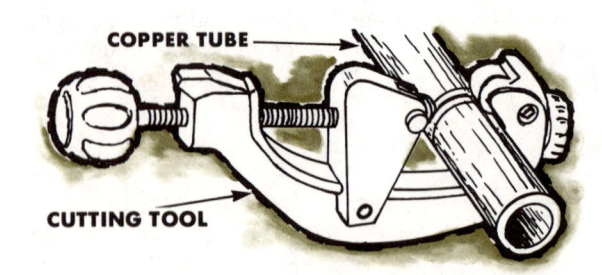

Figure 15-2: A copper tubing cutter makes the cleanest cut. Tighten the handle and rotate the cutter around the pipe. Repeat this process until the pipe is cut through.

to destroy the galvanized pipe within a few weeks. To avoid this eating away, called electrolysis, you must use an insulating union (figure 15-1) or coupling.

You can cut copper tubing with a hacksaw, but you will have to file the edge clean both inside and out. A tubing cutter (figure 15-2) leaves cleaner ends. The reamer on the cutter is used to reshape the turned-in edge. Copper tubing is joined to copper fittings by soldering.

Plastic pipe is becoming more common for replacement pipe. It does not rust or corrode and is not subject to electrolysis. Check your local building code to see if it is permitted in your area.

Plastic pipe is easy to cut with a hacksaw (figure 15-3). Clean the inside edge with a pocket knife and the outside with a file.

Different kinds of plastics are used for pipes. Some are rated for hot water, some for sewers, and some can be used under pressure. Be sure you use the right kind for the job. Cements for joining plastic pipe also vary. Base your choice of cement on the type of pipe you are using.

People have made pipe for thousands of years, but fittings with standard, interchangeable threads are fairly new.

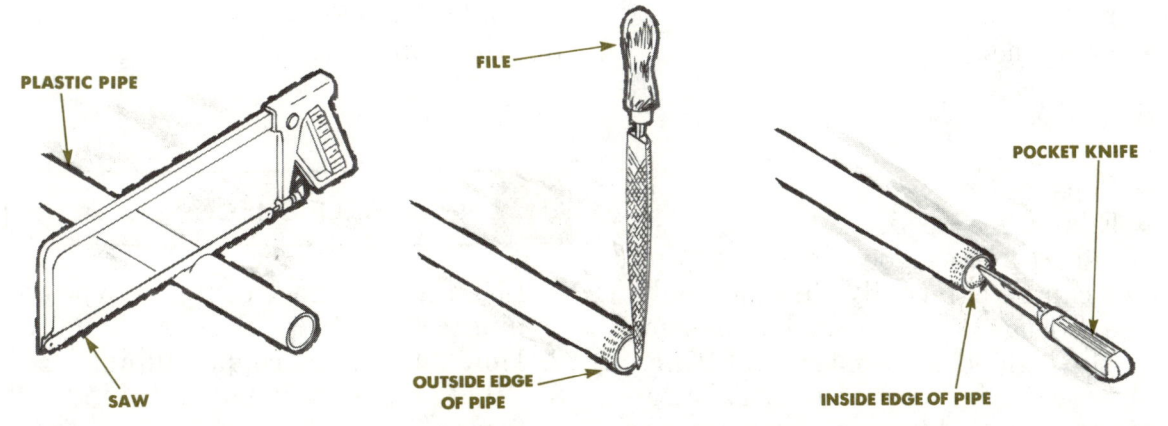

Figure 15-3: Plastic pipe is sawed to length. Then file the outside edge and trim the inside with a pocket knife.

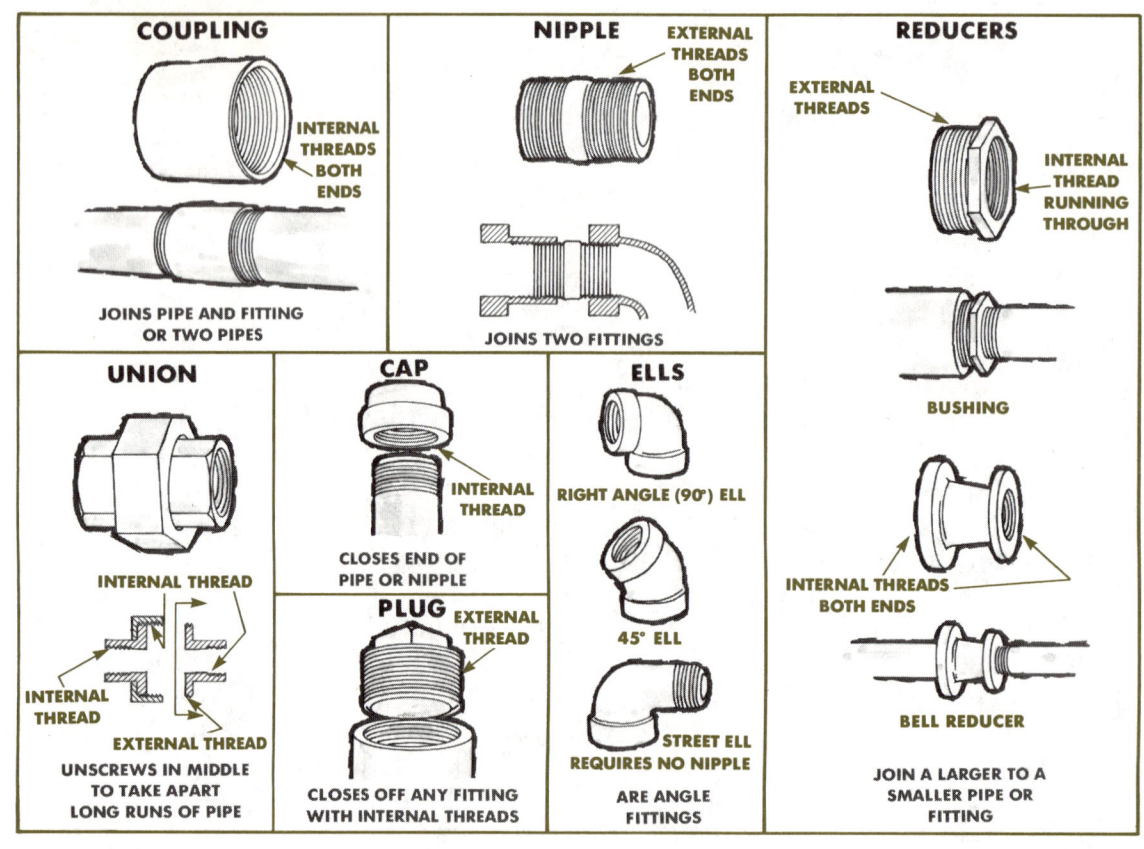

Figure 15-4: Various types of pipe fittings.

Some of the main kinds of fittings (figure 15-4) are:
- Couplings
- Nipples
- Reducers
- Unions
- Caps and plugs
- Ells

No fitting ever goes inside a pipe. Pipes can be externally threaded only. Some fittings are threaded and some are slip (glued or soldered) fittings. There are regular and drainage fittings. The drainage fittings are smoother inside. Choose the right type and the right material for the job. Special fittings can be made by combining these fittings.

SELF CHECK

1. List the five most common types of pipe.
2. How do you cut copper tubing?
3. What are two important kinds of fittings?
4. How do you choose the right fitting?

JOINING PIPE AND TUBING Unit 16

There are four basic ways to join pipe and tubing:
- Pouring lead in the joint
- Screwing together threaded pipes and fittings
- Soldering
- Gluing or cementing

At one time plumbers sealed the joints of black iron pipe with hot, liquid lead. Today, however, sewer pipes are joined with clamps and neoprene gaskets.

Most galvanized pipes are threaded. They can be screwed together without any preparation, but the joint will leak until it rusts shut. It is also very difficult to turn the pipes. Teflon tape makes the job easier and seals the joints as well. Be careful though. Teflon makes the threads turn so easily that you can tighten them too far and break the pipe.

Copper tubing is usually soldered. Clean the joint with steel wool or sandpaper. Do not touch the joint after cleaning. Your fingers may leave some grease that will repel the solder. Apply a light coat of noncorrosive soldering flux to the ends to be joined, both inside and out (figure 16-1). Assemble the joint exactly as it will be when finished.

Now light a propane torch. When

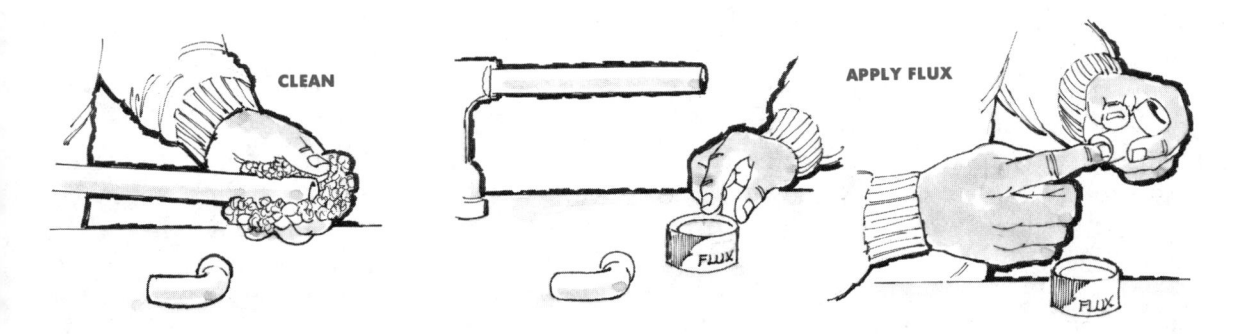

Figure 16-1: Before soldering copper tubing, clean the ends to be joined. Use sandpaper, steel wool, or a wire brush. Then with your finger or with an old toothbrush apply flux to the surfaces being joined. Use a light coat, but cover the area completely.

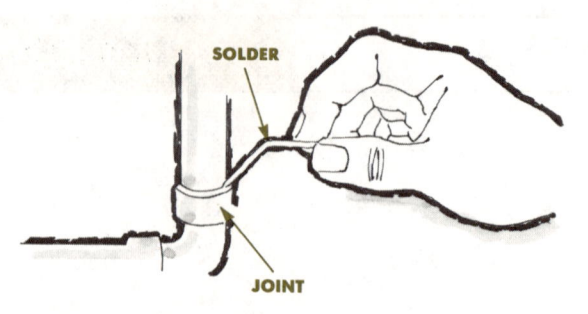

Figure 16-2: If the joint has been properly prepared and heated, it is sufficient to touch the end of the solder to the joint. The solder will melt and flow into the joint.

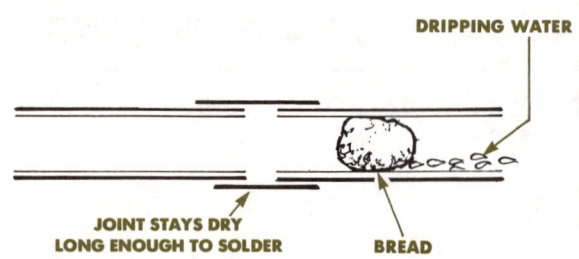

Figure 16-4: To prevent any water from coming in contact with the joint, you may plug the pipe with a piece of bread. The bread will hold the water back long enough for you to solder the joint.

Figure 16-3: If the joint is too hot, solder will not stick. Pull the joint apart and let it cool. Then clean and flux it before beginning again.

the flame settles down, move the torch so the blue tip of the flame is 1/2 to 3/4 inch from the joint. Heat the entire joint and along the tubing for 2 to 3 inches in all directions. Watch where you're pointing the flame. Heat until the flux begins to boil. Do not overheat.

Remove the torch and touch the solder to the end of the joint (figure 16-2). If the joint is clean and fluxed and has been heated to the right temperature, the solder will melt immediately and flow through the whole joint. Do not move the joint until the solder has cooled. If the joint is too hot, the solder will not stick. In this case, use pliers to pull the hot joint apart (figure 16-3). Let it cool, clean it, flux it, and start again.

It is impossible to solder a wet joint. Even a drop of water is too much. If you've turned off all the valves and opened every faucet, and water still trickles through the line, stuff some bread uphill in the line (figure 16-4). This will stop the water long enough to solder. Later when you turn on the water, the bread will dissolve and be flushed out the nearest faucet.

Plastic pipe joints are the same as copper tubing joints except they are cemented instead of being soldered. After cutting and cleaning the edges with a file and knife, brush cement around the outside of the pipe and the inside of the fitting (figure 16-5). Plastic cement is really a solvent that dissolves the plastic surface. When it evaporates (in about 10 seconds) the

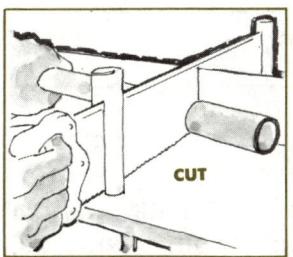

Figure 16-5: To join plastic pipe, cut the pipe, clean the cut edge with a pocket knife, a file, or sandpaper. Brush cement on the outside of the pipe and the inside of the fitting. Join and hold for about ten seconds. There is no way to pull this joint apart again.

joint is fused. This doesn't give you much time to position the joint and wipe away the excess cement. After plastic pipe has been glued, there is no way to take it apart except by cutting.

Use plastic cement with great care. Avoid breathing the fumes and keep it away from eyes, mouth and skin.

SELF CHECK

1. What precaution should you take when using teflon tape?
2. How is copper tubing prepared for soldering?
3. What do you do if solder doesn't stick properly?
4. How can you join plastic pipe?

Unit 17 — SINK AND BASIN TRAPS

When you look at the gooseneck shape of the trap under a sink or basin, it looks as if someone put it there to catch dirt and clog the drain line. It does <u>trap</u> everything from hair to wristwatches. But the real purpose of the trap (figure 17-1) is to keep sewer gas and germs from getting back into the house. Water runs through the trap, but there is always enough left behind in the bottom of the trap to make an airtight seal.

There are four basic ways to clear a clogged trap:
- With a plunger
- With a small plumber's snake
- By removing the cleanout plug if the trap has one
- By removing the trap

The best and safest way of clearing a trap is with a plunger (figure 17-2). Chemicals sometimes work, but when they don't, you have a trap full of a toxic and dangerous substance besides a clogged drain. If the sink has an overflow, as most bathroom basins do, you will have to cover the overflow with a sponge or a rag while you are plunging. Double sinks or laundry basins present a similar problem. Water will be forced through the sink you are not plunging (figure 17-3). Where a plunger won't work, a plumber's snake will sometimes clear the drain. Turn the crank to work it around bends in the pipe.

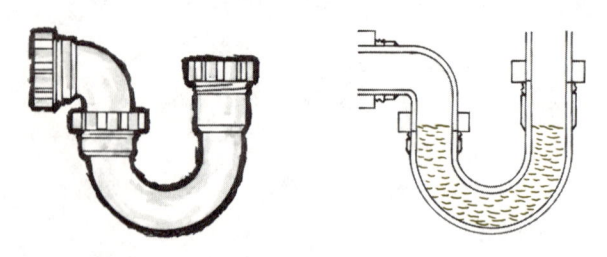

Figure 17-1: Every plumbing fixture—sink, basin, bathtub, toilet and floor drain—has a trap. The trap prevents sewer gas and germs from entering the home.

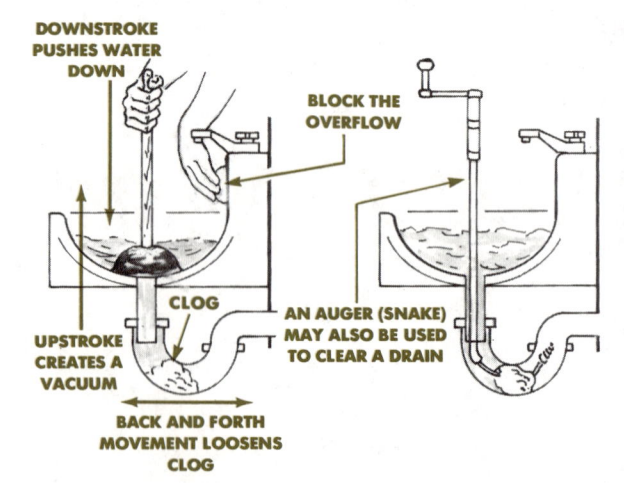

Figure 17-2: To use a plunger put a little petroleum jelly around the force cup to make a tighter seal. Place the plunger over the clogged drain and run two or three inches of water into the sink. Press down firmly on the plunger. As you pull up, a vacuum is created to loosen the clog. If the plunger doesn't work, try a plumber's snake (auger).

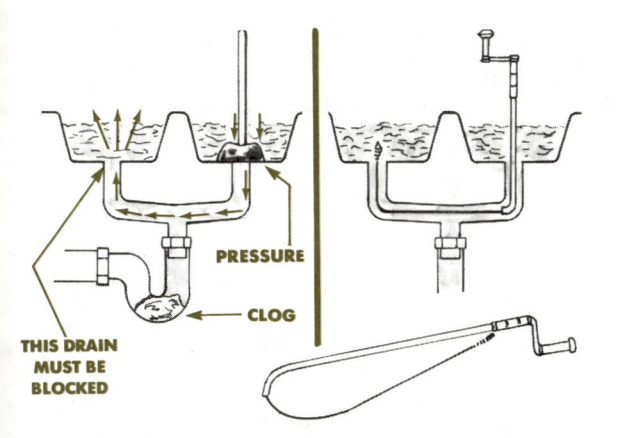

Figure 17-3: Double sinks are connected to the same drain. This may also be true when sinks are back-to-back with a wall between. It is useless to plunge one without blocking the other. One solution may be a plumber's snake (auger).

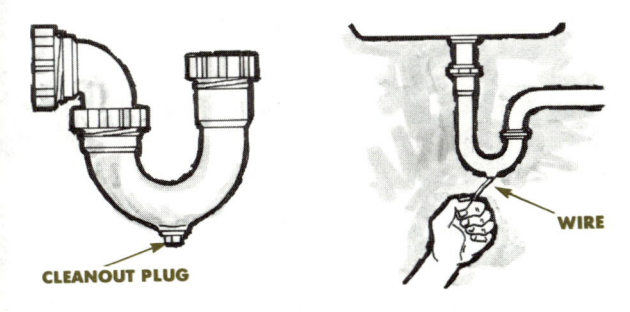

Figure 17-4: A trap with a cleanout plug is fairly easy to clean. Use a piece of wire to break the clog.

Figure 17-5: To remove a trap, put a pail or pan under the trap. Loosen the slip nuts and pull the trap loose. If the trap is not clogged, the problem is farther down the line. Run an auger through the pipe that enters the wall.

Some traps have a cleanout plug (figure 17-4). Put a pail under the trap and remove the plug. Use a piece of stiff wire to clean out the trap. Replace the washer and plug. If that doesn't work or if there is no cleanout plug, remove the trap (figure 17-5). An old trap may be corroded or even fall apart when you remove it. Replace it with a plastic trap. Plastic won't corrode, lasts longer, and is less expensive. If the trap is still usable, run a wire through to clear it.

A little petroleum jelly will help the ends go back together. Tighten the slip nuts by hand and then slightly more with a wrench. Run some water through to make sure there are no leaks.

SELF CHECK

1. What is the purpose of a trap in a sink?
2. What is the best way to clear a clogged trap?
3. Why should you avoid chemicals for unclogging drains?
4. How do you remove a sink trap?

Unit 18   SEWER PIPES

Sewage lines have only two parts:
- Drain pipes
- Vents

Fixtures drain into a straight pipe which empties into a larger pipe. The larger line is made of 4- to 8-inch pipes laid on a slant to carry water and waste into the sewer (figure 18-1).

Vent pipes (figure 18-2) are installed at each drain to let air into the system. Without vents, water would drain very slowly and be pulled out of the traps. Vents also release sewer gas above the level of the house.

To clean a clogged vent, inspect the vent at the roof. Sometimes birds build

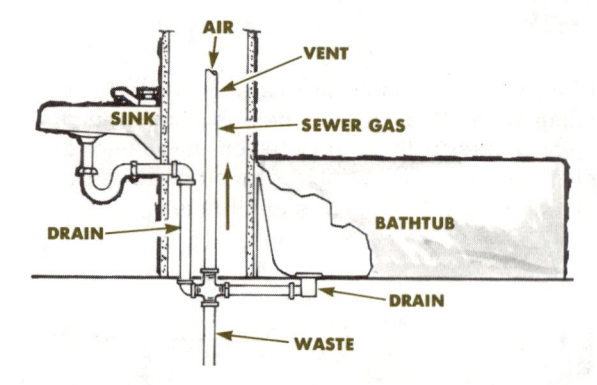

Figure 18-2: Air vents keep water in the traps and help speed up drainage. They also release sewer gas.

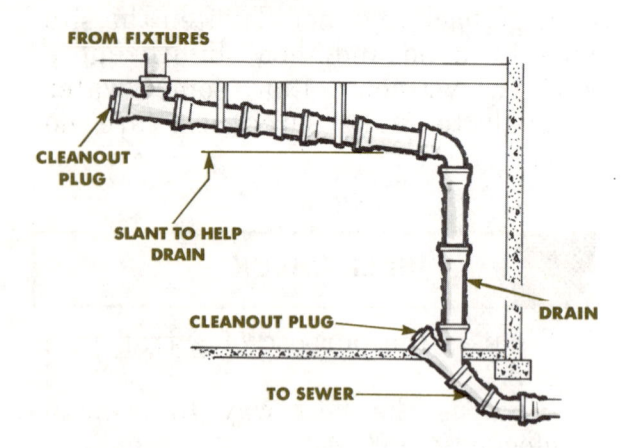

Figure 18-1: The drain system is set up to remove waste quickly and thoroughly. Vertical pipes are placed as straight as possible. Horizontal pipes are slanted toward the sewer.

nests in vents. If that is the case, it is simply a matter of removing the nest. You may have to run a rod or auger down the vent to clear it. Use a cone-shaped cover to keep things from falling in the vent pipe.

Sewer lines have one or more cleanout plugs (figure 18-3) that can be removed. If the clog is near the cleanout you may be able to remove it with a wire or sewer rod. Sometimes a garden hose will work if the water is turned on full force. You can also use an auger (figure 18-4). Heavy-duty ones up to 100 feet long can be rented.

Sewer Pipes 51

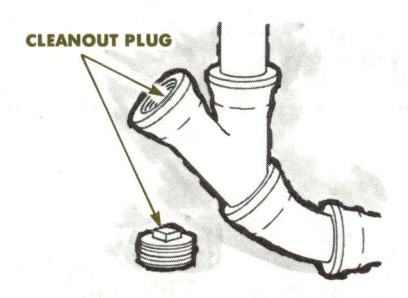

Figure 18-3: Cleanout plugs provide access to drain lines. If water leaks out when you open the plug, the clog is farther along the line. If water does not run out, the clog is between the fixture and the cleanout.

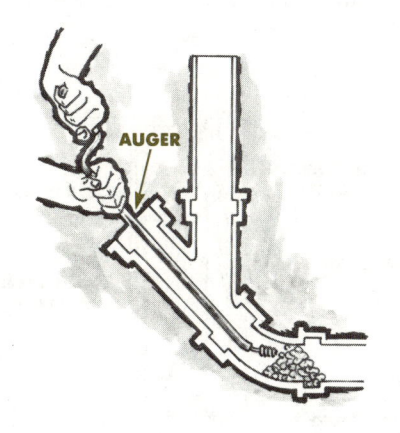

Figure 18-4: An auger or snake may be used to break up the clog.

Occasionally tree roots are attracted to the water in a leaking sewer line and grow into the pipe. You can clear the line with a motorized, heavy-duty auger (figure 18-5). First estimate the distance from the center of the street (where the main sewer line is) to the cleanout plug that is most distant. This is the length of the rooter you will need. Feed the cable until it meets the roots. Then feed slowly as the blade cuts the roots. Flush with a garden hose and run the rooter through again. Remove the rooter and replace the cleanout plug.

SELF CHECK

1. What is the difference between drain lines and vents?
2. How can you tell if the vent is clogged?
3. Where is the main sewer line?
4. How do you use a rooter?

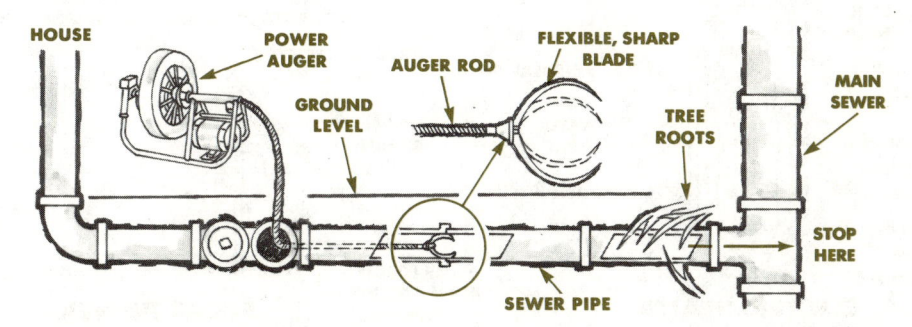

Figure 18-5: A power auger is needed to clear tree roots from a sewer line. Estimate the distance to the main sewer line so you will have an idea of when the rooter has run the entire length of sewer pipe.

Unit 19   WATER HEATERS

Some older houses still heat water by running it through coils in an oil furnace. Some very modern homes use solar energy to heat the water. The most common water heaters are gas or electric (figure 19-1).

Regardless of the type, all water heaters require some maintenance. A leaky water heater should be replaced by a new one. But other problems can be avoided or cured. They include:
- Build up of sediment in the heater
- Top fittings that leak
- Leaky pressure relief valves

Rust or other sediments can build up in the tank. You should drain the tank about once a year to remove them. Turn off the heat, and shut off the

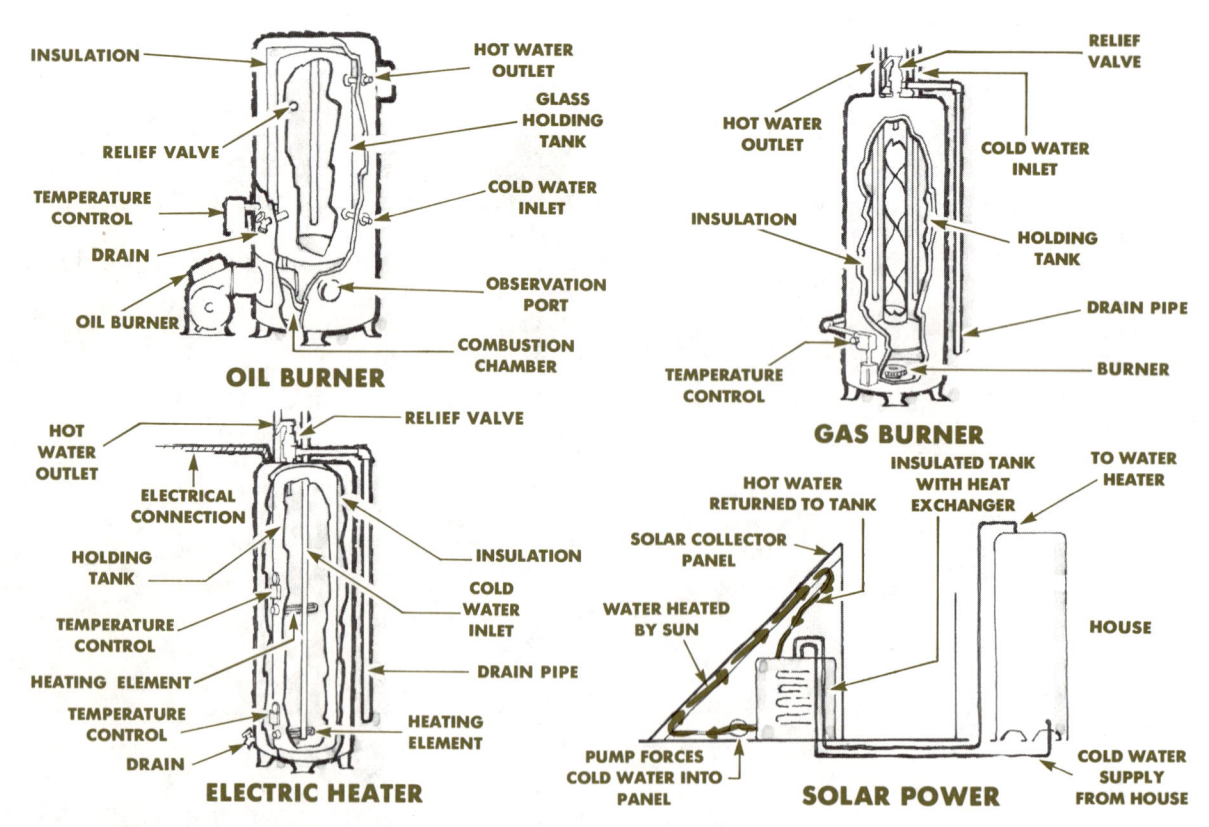

Figure 19-1: All water heaters have the same basic parts: a source of energy, a holding tank, cold water inlet, hot water outlet, a relief valve, drain, and some means of temperature control.

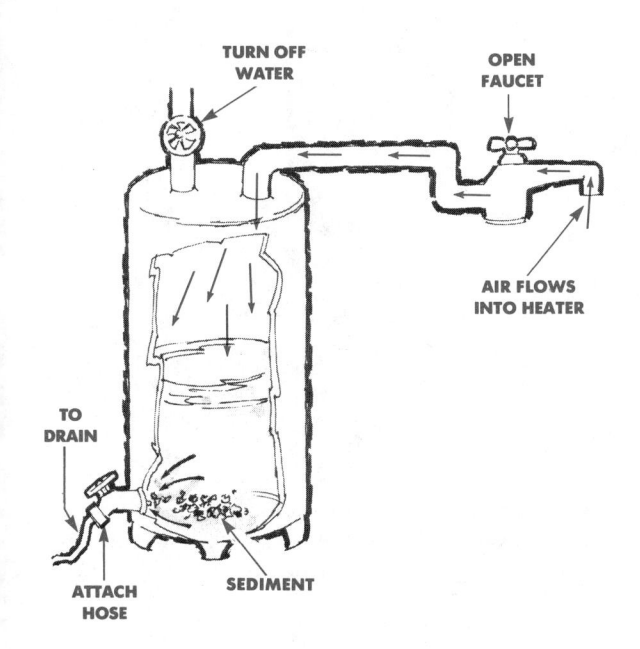

Figure 19-2: Open a hot water faucet to let air into the water heater. Drain and refill the tank. Continue until the water runs clear.

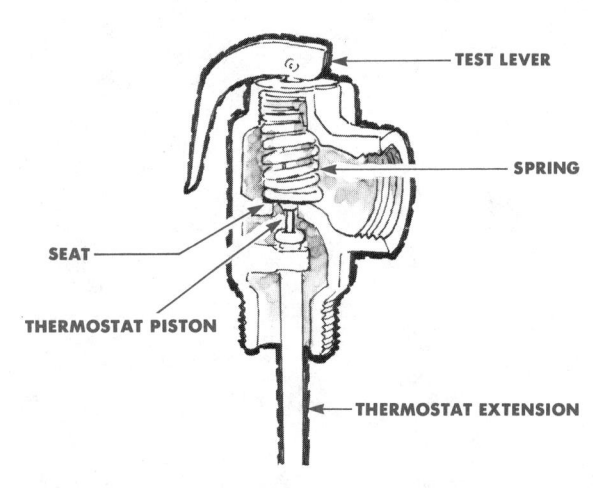

Figure 19-3: Pressure relief valves are spring valves that leak when there is too much pressure in the water heater. This usually happens when there is too much heat or the local water pressure is too high. The cure is to lower the water temperature or install a water pressure regulator between the meter and the house.

water entering the heater. Open any hot water faucet in the house to let in air so the tank will drain. Attach a water hose to the drain spout of the water heater (figure 19-2). Wear gloves because the hose will be too hot to handle. Drain the water into a floor drain or a pail that is lower than the tank spout. When the heater is empty, run more water into it. Keep draining it until the water runs clear.

If the fittings at the top of the tank are made of different metals, electrolysis may cause them to start corroding. An insulated fitting should have been used. Sometimes the fittings can be replaced in time.

Pressure relief valves (figure 19-3) keep the tank from bursting. A leaking pressure valve may mean that the water pressure is too high. This happens when the water is too hot or when there is no regulator between the meter and the house. A leaking pressure relief valve may also be worn out and need replacing.

Gas and oil heaters have some particular problems. If the flame is not a blue color, call the gas or oil company to come and adjust it.

When the pilot light in a gas heater goes out, turn off the gas. Clean around the pilot light and burner with a stiff brush. Vacuum the exhaust vent and

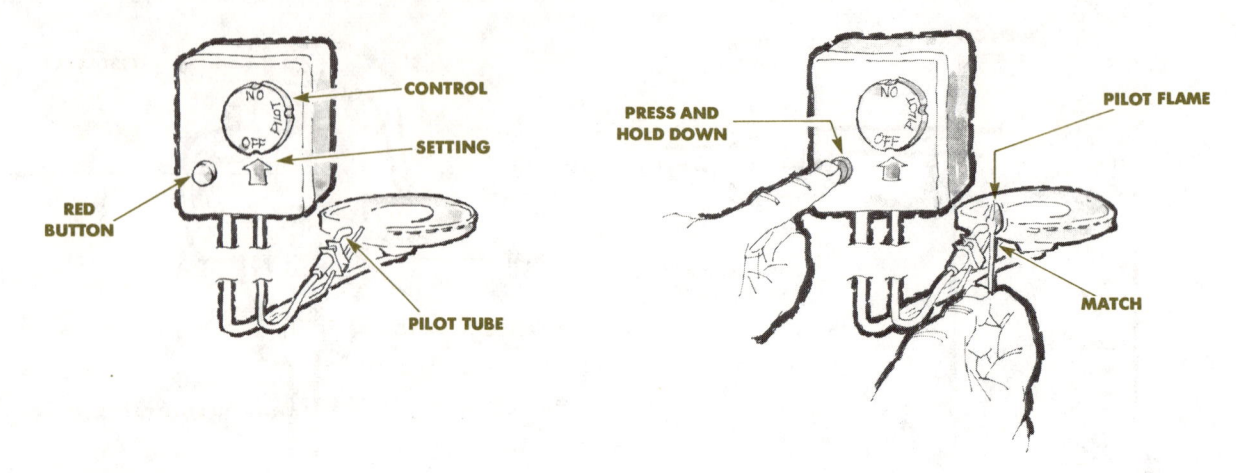

Figure 19-4: Occasionally the pilot light on the water heater goes out. Turn the control to OFF and wait five minutes for any free gas to escape. Then turn the dial to PILOT. Hold the red button down (or the dial if there is no button) and light the pilot. After about a minute the pilot will continue to burn when the button is released. Turn the dial to ON, and the heater should operate normally.

underside of the heater. To light the pilot again (figure 19-4), set the dial to PILOT. Hold the dial or button down, and light the pilot. Keep holding it down until the pilot stays lit. Then turn the dial to ON and set the thermostat.

Water heaters can be made more efficient by wrapping them in a special thermal insulating blanket. You can also save hot water by making sure none of your faucets are leaking.

SELF CHECK

1. When is it necessary to replace a hot water heater?
2. How do you get rusty water out of a water heater?
3. What color should a gas water heater flame burn?
4. What are some ways to improve your hot water system?

HEATING AND AIR CONDITIONING   Unit 20

Homes are heated by one of three methods:
- Hot water
- Steam
- Warm air

Hot water systems use a pump to circulate hot water from a boiler to all the rooms in a house (figure 20-1). Keep the radiators clean and the tops uncovered so that heat can circulate. About once a year, drain the boiler and expansion tank. Turn off the burner and the water coming into the tank. The process is the same as flushing a hot water tank. Attach a hose to the drain and open the vents on the highest radiators to let in air. After the water runs clear, close the drain and open the water supply. Relight the burner. When you hear water entering the radiators, close the vents again.

Refilling the tank will let air in. As the air rises it becomes trapped in the radiator and keeps the water from circulating. You will have to "bleed" each radiator. This is done by opening the radiator to let out the air (figure 20-2). As soon as water comes out, close the radiator. Be careful when catching the water. It will be hot.

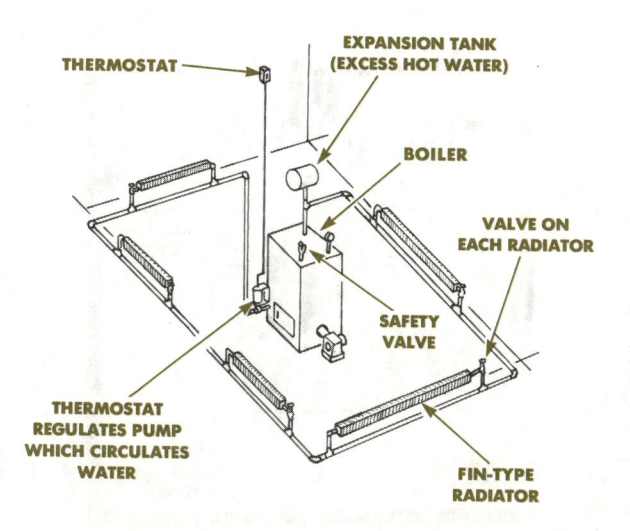

Figure 20-1: A hot water system is controlled by a thermostat. The thermostat controls an electric pump which circulates water throughout the house.

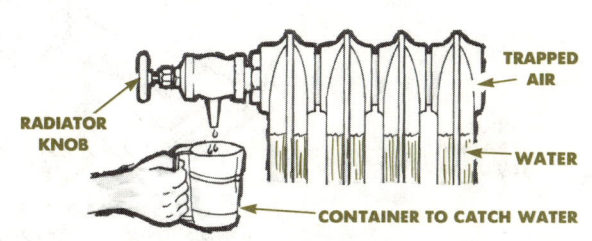

Figure 20-2: Bleed the radiator of trapped air by opening the knob until water just begins to trickle out. Be careful: the water will be hot.

A steam system is similar to the hot water system. It does not have a pump though, because the steam circulates freely. Noises occur when water becomes trapped in pipes that do not slope back toward the boiler. This may be cured with a block of wood under one leg of the radiator (figure 20-3). Knocking may also occur if the steam valve is not fully open or closed.

Loose packing in a valve is often responsible for steam leaking. This can be repaired just as you would a faucet (figure 20-4). Turning down the packing nut may stop the leak. If not, repack the stem.

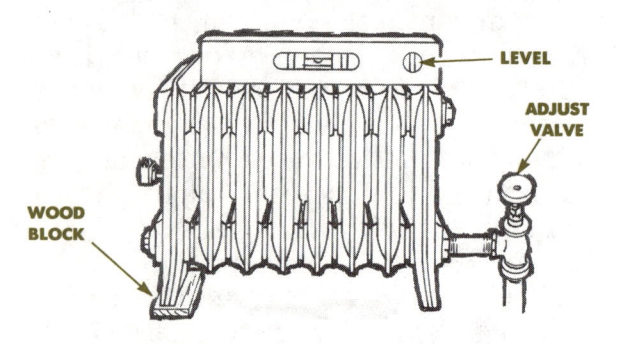

Figure 20-3: To stop radiator pounding make sure the pipes are level so water is not trapped. Also try adjusting the valve.

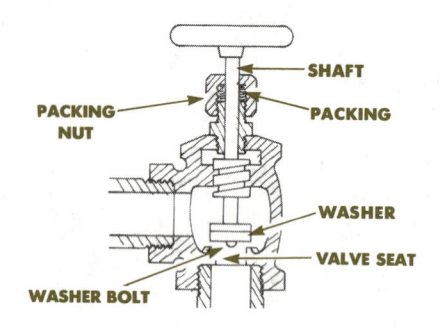

Figure 20-4: Make repairs with the furnace off and the boiler cold. If steam leaks out the radiator valve, tighten the packing nut. If that doesn't work, remove the packing nut and repack the stem with packing cord. Reassemble the valve.

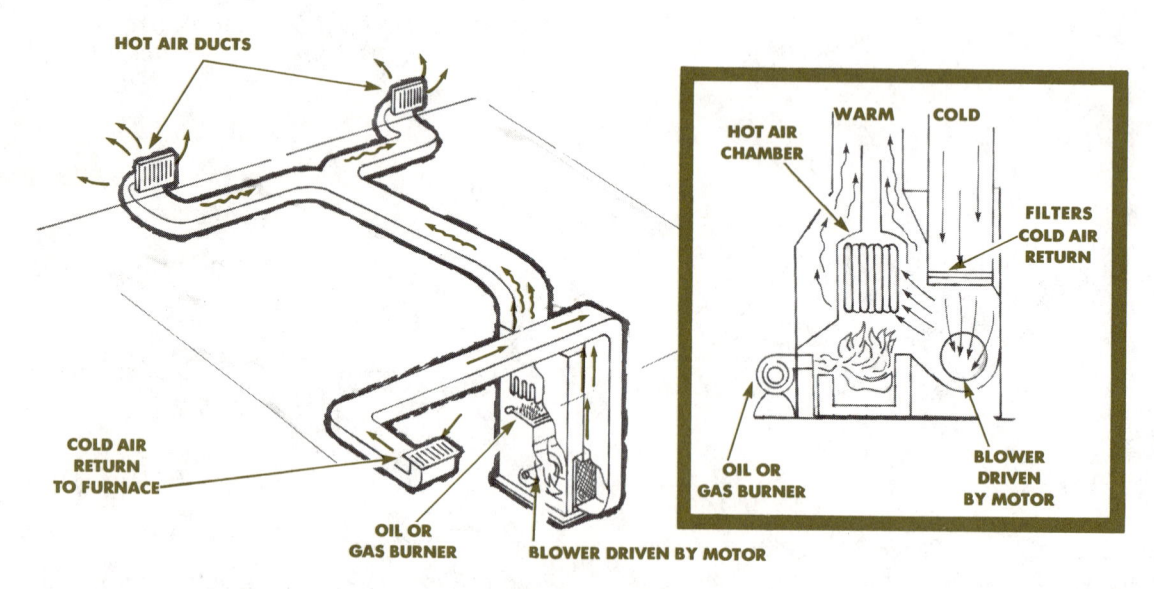

Figure 20-5: A warm air heating system heats air and blows it through heating ducts. The air can be heated by oil or gas burners.

Basically a warm air furnace heats air which is circulated by a blower. Warm air systems may be electric, gas, or fuel oil heated. Heated air travels through ducts and out through grills or registers in various rooms (figure 20-5). As with the other systems, a warm-air system must be kept clean. Clean or change the filters monthly when the heater is in use. Change them at least once a year. Also clean the fan blades and vacuum around the registers. If necessary, tighten the belt.

The motors in all systems need oiling. Use a lightweight motor oil and fill the cups or filling tubes in the motor. Fans and water pump bearings need oiling as well. If pipes or ducts run through cold areas, they should be insulated.

Central air conditioning may operate through the heating ducts. However, many homes have individual room air conditioners. The main thing is to keep the filters clean when the air conditioner is in use.

SELF CHECK

1. How do you bleed a radiator?
2. What are two possible ways to stop pounding noises in a steam heating system?
3. How often should a warm air heating filter be changed?
4. What should be done to keep air conditioners running efficiently?

4 FINISHING WALLS

Walls are the first thing anyone entering your home will see. They should be kept clean and in good repair.

There are many ways to finish walls. Probably the most common is painting. Paint preserves and beautifies many objects. It protects metal from rust, wood from mildew and plastics from sun damage. Paint also makes them easier to clean.

There are many types of wall coverings. Paper, plastics, and fabrics are some. Wall coverings can be prepasted and pretrimmed. Some are washable; and some are even treated for easy removal at a later date.

Paneling is easy to care for, and there are many different types to choose from.

Whatever type of wall finish you use, the job should be clean and neat. You should also know some of the chemistry of the materials and surfaces you are working with—what will mix and what may explode.

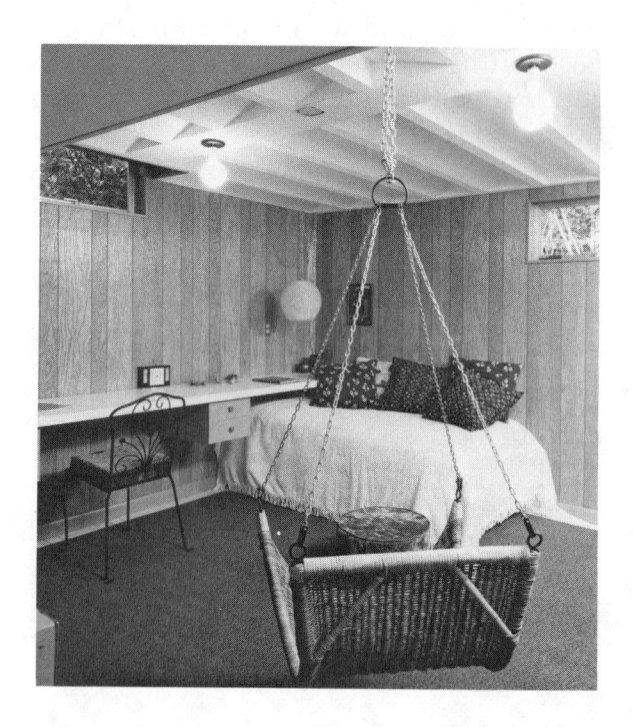

Painters will always have work. Even if the perfect paint—one that never wears out—is discovered, there will always be someone who doesn't like the color!

CEILINGS AND WALLS — Unit 21

In many modern houses, interiors are finished with drywall. Drywall normally comes in sheets, 4' x 8', 4' x 10', or 4' x 12'. It is usually 5/16, 3/8, 1/2 or 5/8 inch thick. The most common size is 3/8 inch thick 4' x 8'.

Drywall sheets are nailed to the house joists with large headed nails, screws, or staples (figure 21-1). Nails are driven so that a small dent is made in the drywall (figure 21-2). This depression is then filled with a type of cement and covered over with tape (figure 21-3).

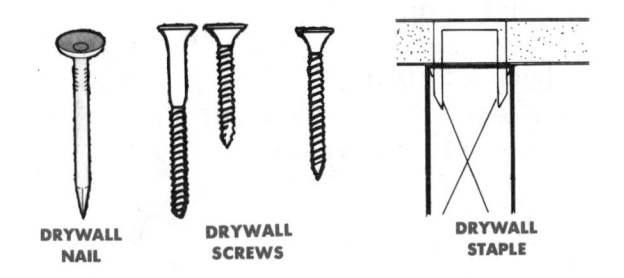

Figure 21-1: Drywall is soft. It is best held in place with large headed drywall nails, screws or staples.

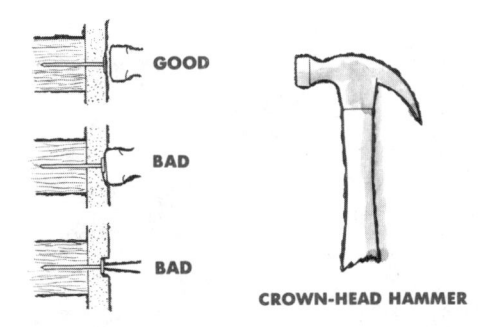

Figure 21-2: To prevent nails and seams from showing, nails are dented into the walls. The dents are then filled with drywall cement. Then you cover the seams with drywall tape and plaster over with drywall cement.

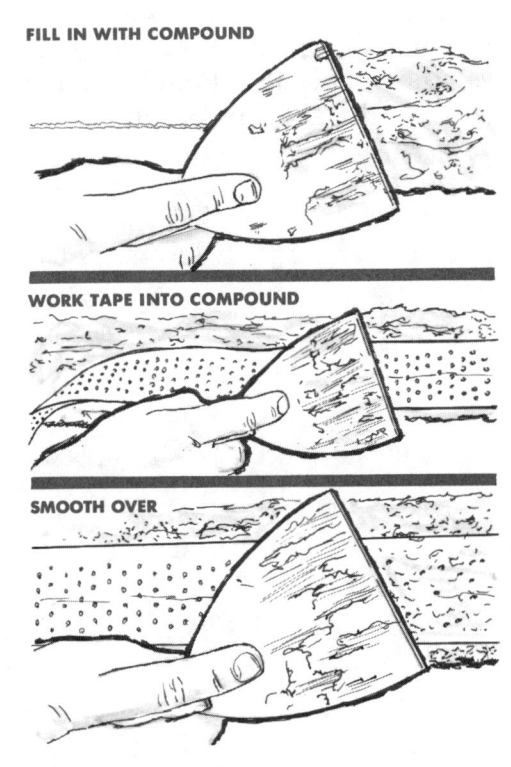

Figure 21-3: Finishing drywall seams. Apply compound over the seams and nail impressions. Work the tape into this compound. Smooth over, allow to dry, and sand.

There are three basic ways to finish drywall:
- Painting
- Wallpapering
- Paneling

You may apply paint directly to drywall. New drywall usually takes two coats: one to seal it and one to present an even, finished surface.

Wallpaper is becoming popular again. It comes in rolls and is applied directly to the drywall. Before it will stick, the drywall must be prepared with a glue-like coating of sizing. The trick in applying wallpaper is to avoid bubbles and match the edges and the pattern precisely.

Paneling is glued or nailed directly onto the drywall. Panels may be veneer, wallboard, imitation masonry, or some other material.

Moldings and baseboards finish off walls and ceilings. In older homes they are always made of wood. Most new molding and baseboard is made of synthetic materials which are more flexible and less likely to crack when nailed into place.

SELF CHECK

1. Why should you leave a dent when driving drywall nails?
2. In what three ways are walls commonly finished?
3. How should drywall be treated before finishing?
4. Why are baseboards made of synthetic materials?

WALL REPAIRS Unit 22

Older walls and sometimes even new ones will need some repair before finishing. The most common wall repairs include:
- Dents
- Small holes
- Large holes
- Nail pops
- Split tape

You can repair dents by sanding around them, trowling joint compound (spackle) into the dent, and finally smoothing out the area. This is essentially plastering (figure 22-1). Once it is dry, you can sand, seal, paint, or wallpaper the patch to match the rest of the wall.

Small holes are repaired like dents. A wad of newspaper behind the hole will prevent the joint compound from falling between the walls (figure 22-2).

For large holes, you will have to patch a piece of drywall into place. Remove all loose material from around the hole with a utility knife. Then cut a piece of drywall to fill the hole (figure 22-3). If the patch doesn't rest on solid wood, set a screw in the patch to use as a handle. After the joint compound hardens, remove the screw and plaster

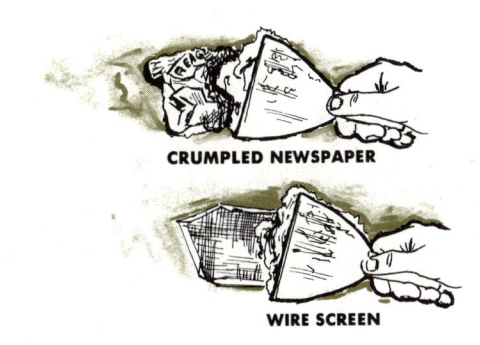

Figure 22-2: Sometimes it is necessary to back a hole with newspaper when filling a hole with spackle or patching plaster. A piece of wire screen or plasterboard works well also.

SAND SO THAT COMPOUND WILL ADHERE

FILL IN WITH JOINT COMPOUND

WHEN DRY, SAND AGAIN

Figure 22-1: Most wall repair is essentially plastering. On drywall, use drywall cement or spackle to fill the hole. Wood walls are repaired with wood putty.

CLEAN EDGES OF HOLE AND CUT NEW PATCH; APPLY JOINT COMPOUND **HOLD IN PLACE WITH A SCREW** **WHEN DRY, REMOVE SCREW AND FINISH ENTIRE AREA**

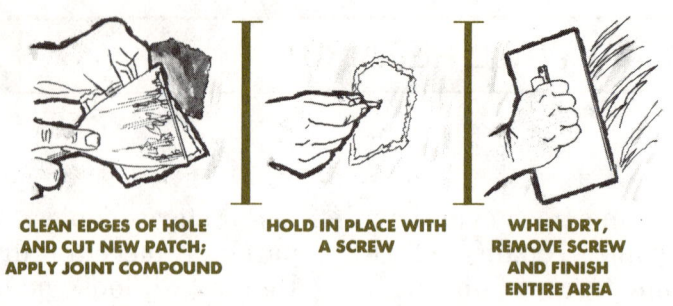

Figure 22-3: Repair large holes by cutting a piece of drywall to fit the hole. Cement the patch and hold it in place with a handle made from a screw. When it has dried, remove the screw and plaster, sand and finish the whole area.

the whole patch with joint cement. Then sand the patch to match the rest of the wall.

When the house framing expands or shrinks, nails pop and become visible under the paint or wallpaper. If the nails are tight, just drive them back below the surface with a claw hammer. Plaster the dent with joint compound. If the nails are loose, pull them if it won't damage the wall, or drive them so deep they won't come out again. Then drive new nails nearby. Cover the nails with joint cement (figure 22-4). Use only drywall nails. Regular nails will rust when covered with joint cement.

Split tape is caused by the house settling. The tape will bulge like a bubble or blister or actually crack. Cut and pull off the loose tape. Remove all the loose tape or it will split again. Then sand the area and spread a thin coat of joint compound over it. With a wide putty knife work the tape into this compound (figure 22-5). Plaster over the tape with compound. When it is dry, sand it.

Bathroom and kitchen walls are sometimes covered with ceramic tile. When a tile is cracked, it should be replaced. Start by removing the tile and old grout. You may have to break the tile with a hammer and chisel.

POPPED NAIL **POUND NAIL BACK WITH NAIL SET** **POUND NEW NAILS CLOSE TO THE OLD** **COVER THE DENT WITH JOINT COMPOUND** **SAND**

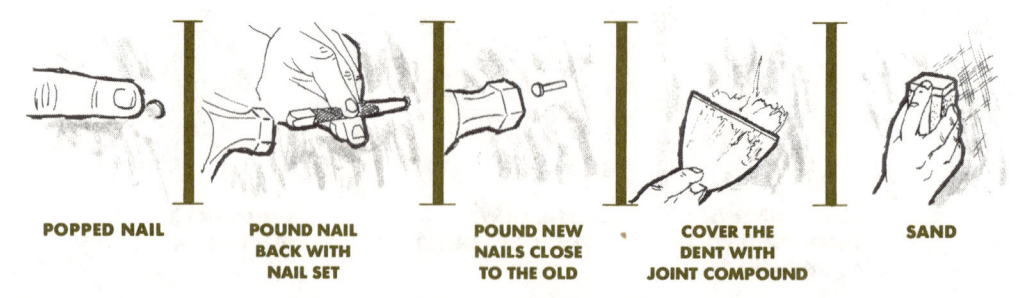

Figure 22-4: Nail pops that are tight can simply be driven back in with a hammer and a nail set. Loose nails should be pulled or driven in. Drive a new nail nearby.

Wall Repairs

Figure 22-5: Remove all tape that is loose. Spread joint compound over the area and work new tape down with a putty knife. Then plaster over.

Although the tile is usually set in a special cement, it is much easier to glue the replacement tile with white epoxy cement. The wall must be dry. Use a putty knife or cover your finger with a piece of plastic or cellophane and work the epoxy around the tile to match the old grout (figure 22-6). Hold the tile in place until the epoxy begins to set.

Figure 22-6: Gluing tiles with white epoxy cement is easier than using grout. The cement must be spread by hand to look like grout. Protect your finger with a piece of plastic.

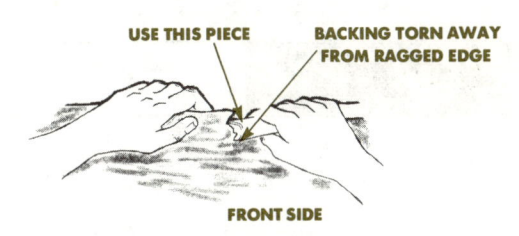

Figure 22-7: An uneven piece of wallpaper is less noticeable than one that is cut straight. Tearing the backing off the edges will make it even less obvious.

Clean all cement off the tiles before it hardens.

Wallpaper is difficult to repair. To replace a greasy or torn spot, carefully tear a piece of matching wallpaper from the front of the patch so the backing will be torn away from the edges (figure 22-7). Remove the old piece. Match the pattern and paste down the new patch. The seams will always be slightly visible, but the ragged edges will make them less obvious.

Sometimes wallpaper bulges loose in a bubble. Cut a small slit in the bubble and force paste behind it, in order to work the bubble down. The cut is less visible if it is made along a straight line in the wallpaper pattern.

SELF CHECK

1. How would you repair a dent or small hole in drywall?
2. What is the best way to repair a large hole?
3. How would you treat nail pops?
4. How can you repair a wallpaper bubble?

Unit 23 — PAINT SAFETY

Painting can be dangerous. The careless use and storage of paints and related materials can cause needless injuries. Safe painting has two aspects:
- Safety of the painter and other people
- Safety of property

Most important, of course, is personal safety. This includes using a ladder properly. First inspect the ladder. <u>Never</u> use a ladder that is cracked or broken. A ladder should never be painted because paint may cover a dangerous crack. Place the ladder on a firm base and at the proper slant (figure 23-1).

Personal safety also includes proper use of chemicals such as:
- Cleansers
- Paints
- Thinners

Many of the cleansers used to prepare surfaces for painting are caustic. That means they will burn flesh and often ruin clothing. All dangerous cleansers have warning labels (figure 23-2). Such labels warn against getting the cleanser on your skin, in your eyes, swallowing it, or using it without adequate ventilation. The labels will tell you what to do if one of these things happens. Read the entire warning label <u>before</u> you use the product.

Once the surface is ready, there are more labels to read. Paints and thinners also have directions and warning labels that must be read.

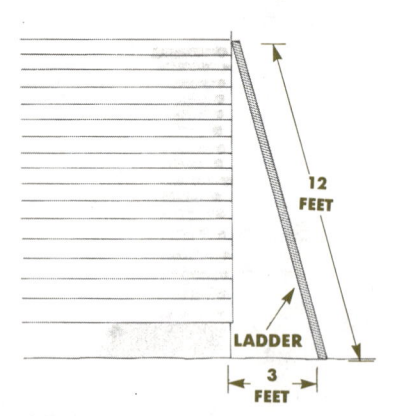

Figure 23-1: Set the ladder on a firm surface so it does not slip. The best angle is made by placing the base of the ladder from the wall a distance of ¼ the ladder's length. Do not climb too high or reach out too far.

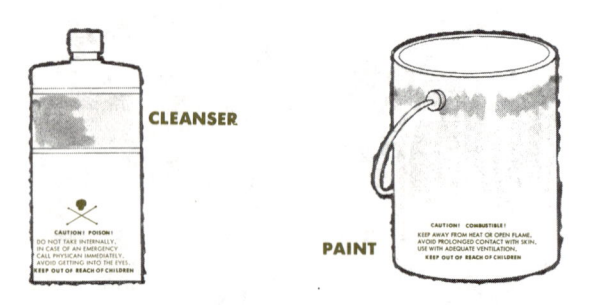

Figure 23-2: Read the entire label before using any caustic chemical such as cleanser, paint, or thinner.

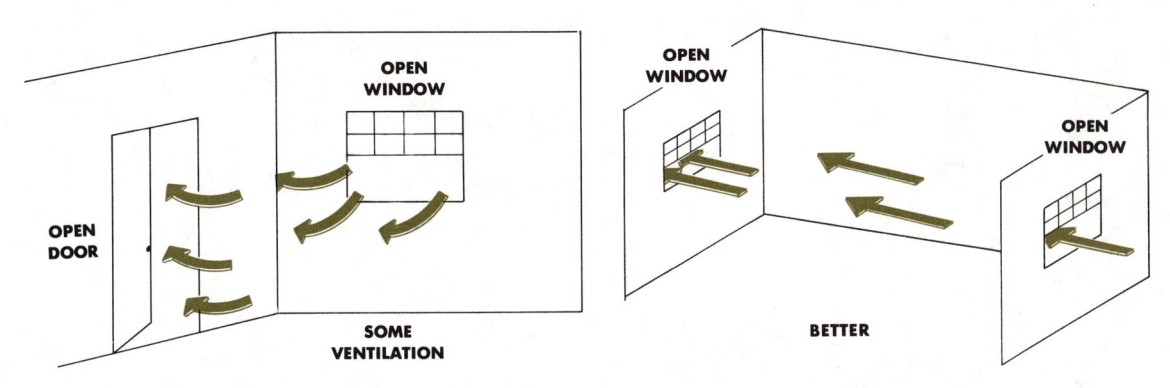

Figure 23-3: Whenever you paint indoors be sure to ventilate the room. Openings at opposite sides of the room are better than two openings in the same area.

Use the correct thinner for the paint you are using. The wrong thinner can make your paint and brush as hard as concrete. Paint thinner, mineral spirits, or turpentine is used to thin and clean up oil based paints. Alcohol dissolves shellac. Lacquer thinner will cut lacquer.

All paint thinners have one thing in common: they evaporate fast. This means that thinner gets into the air where it is easy to breathe. Besides being dangerous to your health, thinner mixed with air is explosive. One spark can set it off.

Always ventilate the working area. Open at least two doors or windows, on opposite walls if possible (figure 23-3). Leave them open until the paint has dried.

Fire is another threat. Under certain conditions some stored chemicals can explode into flames. This is called spontaneous combustion. All flammable materials should be kept in airtight containers to prevent spontaneous combustion.

Paints can also be dangerous. Lead based paint is poisonous, and most states have outlawed the use of lead in paints. Never use paint with lead in it.

Spraying is one of the best and one of the most dangerous ways to apply paint. Always wear a face mask when spray painting (figure 23-4). Be especially careful where you use a

Figure 23-4: Keep chemical containers closed tightly when not in use. Store them in fireproof cabinets. Place rags in fireproof metal containers. Dispose of chemical soaked rags as soon as possible.

spray gun. Sprayed paints can drift a long way (figure 23-5), and it doesn't take much to ruin the paint on a car or nearby house. Spray paint doesn't just disappear into the air. Sooner or later it lands somewhere.

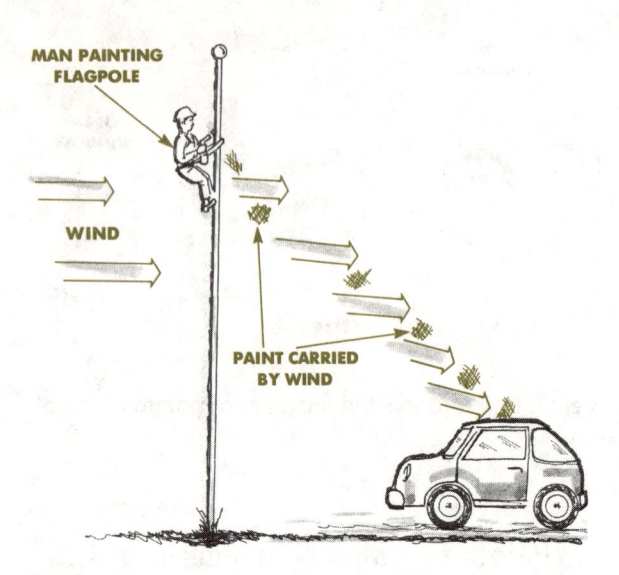

Figure 23-5: Property is often damaged because painters forget how far sprayed paint can be carried by the wind.

SELF CHECK

1. What is a caustic chemical?
2. Why is evaporated thinner dangerous?
3. What is spontaneous combustion?
4. Why can spray paint be dangerous?

PREPARING WALLS FOR PAINT — Unit 24

Applying the paint is the smallest part of a paint job. The real work is in preparing the surface and cleaning up afterward. Before you begin to paint:
- Wash the surface
- Remove any fixtures
- Fill depressions
- Sand smooth
- Prime the surface

First, protect furniture, floors, or shrubs with drop cloths. Knock loose dirt and paint off exterior walls with a high pressure hose. Remove all flaking paint with a scraper or a wire brush.

Interior walls that are already painted are usually washed with trisodium phosphate (TSP) and a stiff brush. TSP is a caustic powder that must be mixed with water (one tablespoonful to a gallon of water). Be sure to wear rubber gloves (figure 24-1). TSP removes skin almost as fast as it removes dirt and grease from old paint. Then rinse the walls with water and dry completely.

Fixtures are removed to make it easier to paint and to keep from getting paint on the fixtures. Remove switch plates only after the wall has been washed. After the switch plates are removed, you may find dirty rings on the wall. This should be carefully wiped off (figure 24-2). Wring your sponge as dry as possible.

Figure 24-1: Mix one tablespoon of trisodium phosphate (TSP) per gallon of water to clean walls before painting. <u>Wear rubber gloves.</u>

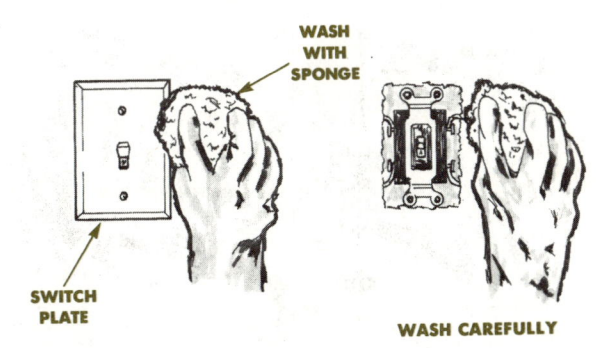

Figure 24-2: After you remove the switch plate, carefully wipe away the ring left on the wall. Do not touch the switch.

SPACKLE OR WOOD PUTTY

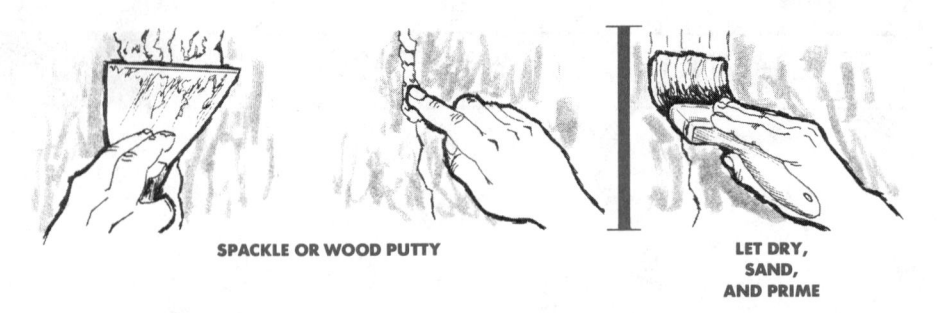

LET DRY, SAND, AND PRIME

Figure 24-3: Fill cracks, holes and dents with the proper filler. Spackle fills holes and cracks that paint cannot cover. A good spackling job makes the difference between a smooth professional job and the kind you'd rather not talk about.

Most walls have cracks, nail holes, or dents. Fill them with wood putty, spackling compound, or another fill, depending on the material the wall is made of (figure 24-3). Before applying spackle, wet the area. Build up the patch slightly above the wall. When it is dry, sand the patch until it is even with the rest of the wall (figure 24-4). Old painted wood must be sanded smooth.

The final step, priming, prepares the surface for paint. Prime patches and seal wood knots with shellac or sealer. Use primer over new wood because new wood absorbs paint like a sponge.

Everything must be thoroughly dry before you begin to paint. There is a lot of work in preparing to paint, but the results are worth it.

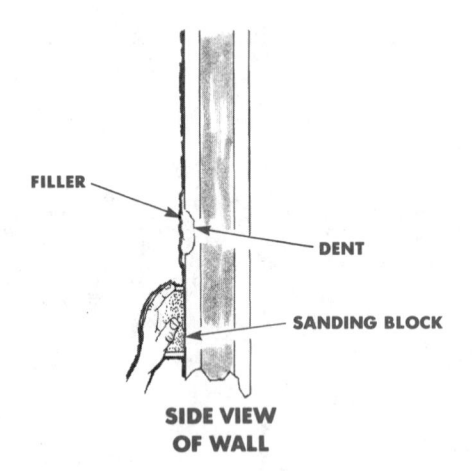

Figure 24-4: Build up patches above the surface. Let them dry, and sand the patch flush with the surface.

SELF CHECK

1. How do you prepare a wall surface for painting?
2. Why are rubber gloves needed when you use TSP?
3. How should holes in the wall be repaired?
4. Why is primer used on new wood?

MIXING PAINT Unit 25

Before you open the paint, gather at least three times as many rags and more thinner than you think you'll need. There will be spills to wipe up and brushes or rollers to clean.

Painting begins with stirring. All paint is made of tiny grains of solid material suspended in a binder. If a can of paint sits long enough, the solid particles will settle to the bottom (figure 25-1).

Paint can be divided into three basic types:
- Paint
- Enamel or varnish
- Lacquer

Paint has a flat finish. Some types, like vinyl, latex, whitewash and kalsomine, clean up with water. Other paints have an oil base and use other solvents like turpentine or mineral spirits.

Painters used to stir new paint by hand with a wooden paddle. Then they strained it through cheesecloth to remove hard lumps. Now most paint stores will mix the paint for you in a machine (figure 25-2). This distributes color evenly.

The only paint you will have to stir is leftover paint. With a stick, lift off the dried paint (the skin) that has formed on top. Wrap it in old newspaper and throw it away.

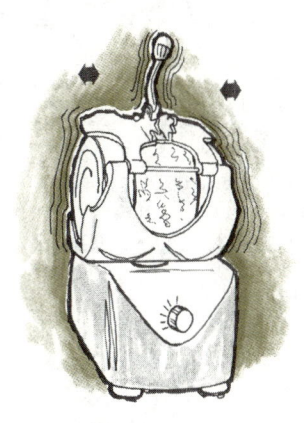

Figure 25-2: Most paint stores have paint mixers to shake up the paint. This method is better and quicker than stirring with a stick.

Figure 25-1: In time paint will separate. It should be thoroughly mixed before being used.

THINNER AND OIL BINDER FLOATS ON TOP

PIGMENT SETTLES TO THE BOTTOM

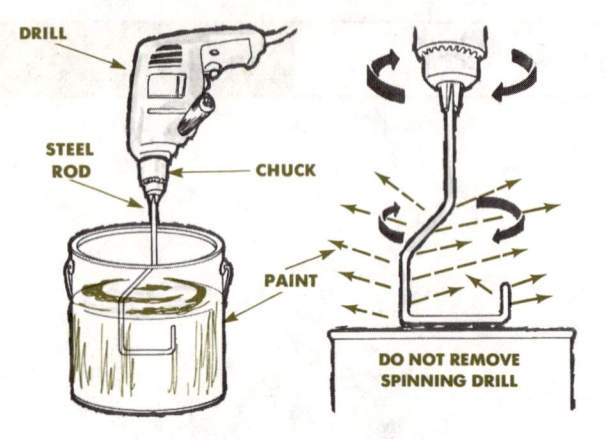

Figure 25-3: A straight steel rod can be bent into a stirrer that can be used in a hand drill. The drill must be off before placing the stirrer into or removing it from the paint can. Steady the paint can with your feet.

Figure 25-4: Shaking enamel, varnish or lacquer creates a foam that will show up as bubbles on the finished surface. NEVER SHAKE ENAMEL, VARNISH, OR LACQUER.

You can make a handy stirrer by bending a piece of steel rod (figure 25-3). Attach it to an electric drill with a chuck. Place the rod all the way into the paint before starting the drill. Do not remove the rod while it is moving. Use this stirrer in an open area where nothing important will get spattered.

Enamel is paint mixed with varnish. It gives a glossy, easy-to-clean surface. Never shake enamel or varnish. Stir it slowly. Shaking will fill the can with bubbles which will show up on the painted surface (figure 25-4). Once enamel or lacquer has been shaken, it will take about a week for the bubbles to disappear.

Lacquer is of a different chemical family. It can't be mixed with anything. If lacquer is painted over enamel, it will soften the enamel like paint remover. However, enamel can be painted over well-dried lacquer. Lacquer, like enamel and varnish, should not be shaken. Industry is the biggest user of lacquer.

When you have all the necessary materials together, you are ready to apply the paint.

SELF CHECK

1. What is the difference between paint and enamel?
2. How did painters mix paint years ago?
3. How do you use a drill and rod stirrer?
4. Why should enamel and varnish not be mixed by shaking?

PAINTING METHODS Unit 26

For thousands of years, natural fiber or animal hair brushes were the only things you could use to paint with. Now, however, there are several ways to apply paint:
- Brushes
- Rollers
- Pads
- Spray guns or cans

Good brushes are expensive, but they hold and distribute paint more evenly than cheap ones. The end of each bristle in a good brush is split or "flagged" (figure 26-1). These "flags" help spread the paint evenly.

FLAG END   BRISTLE

Figure 26-1: Good brushes have bristles with flag ends that hold paint and spread it evenly. Hog bristles make some of the best brushes.

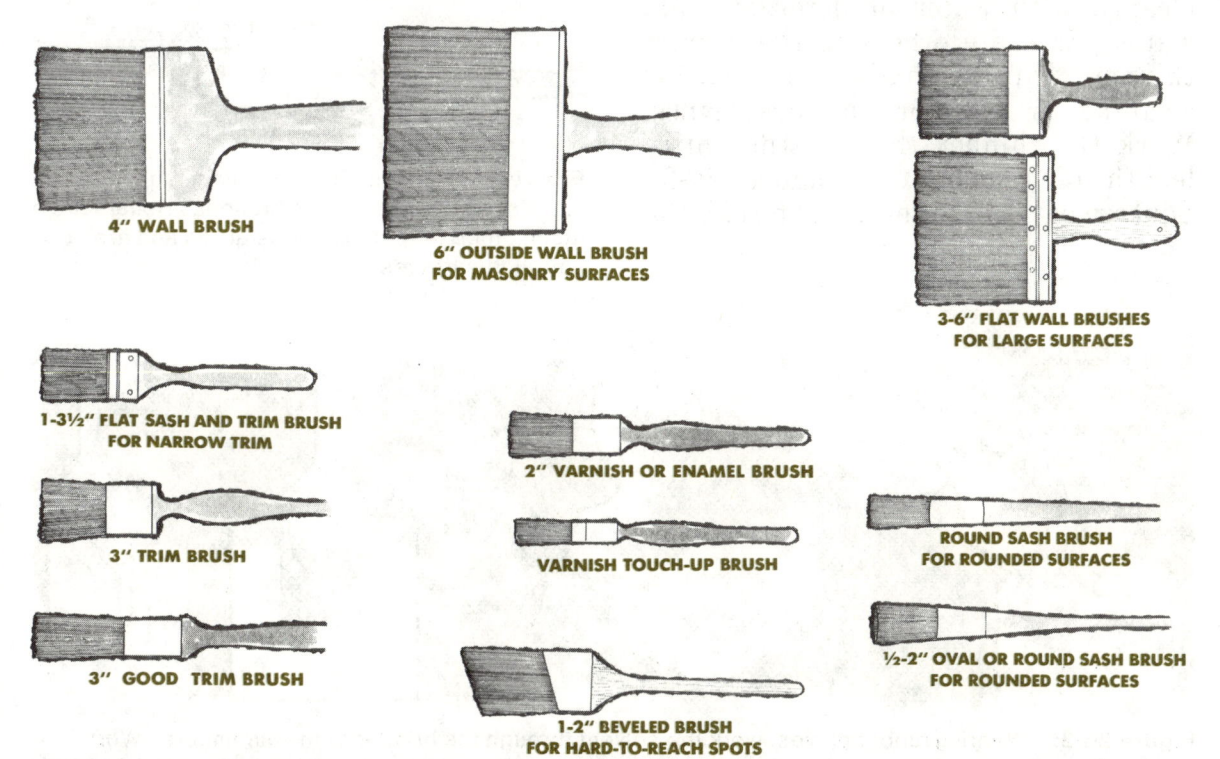

4" WALL BRUSH

6" OUTSIDE WALL BRUSH FOR MASONRY SURFACES

3-6" FLAT WALL BRUSHES FOR LARGE SURFACES

1-3½" FLAT SASH AND TRIM BRUSH FOR NARROW TRIM

3" TRIM BRUSH

3" GOOD TRIM BRUSH

2" VARNISH OR ENAMEL BRUSH

VARNISH TOUCH-UP BRUSH

1-2" BEVELED BRUSH FOR HARD-TO-REACH SPOTS

ROUND SASH BRUSH FOR ROUNDED SURFACES

½-2" OVAL OR ROUND SASH BRUSH FOR ROUNDED SURFACES

Figure 26-2: Brushes come in many sizes and shapes. They are designed for different purposes and for use with different types of paints and finishes.

Natural bristle brushes are used for varnish and oil base paint. For water base paint, use nylon (synthetic) bristles.

The right amount of paint brushed on a wall should cover well but not run. Too much paint should be brushed out evenly before it runs. Too little paint will require a second coat.

Brushes come in several sizes and shapes for different uses (figure 26-2). They may be large and rough for whitewashing, or small and angled to paint around the edges of doors and window frames.

Be sure to clean your brush immediately after you use it. Brushes used for vinyl or latex paints can be cleaned with water or detergent and water. Saturate others in the correct thinner. Thinner that's been used for cleaning is fine for the first rinse. Work the thinner through the entire length of the bristles (figure 26-3). Squeeze out the thinner. Then soak the brush in clean thinner. Work it through again. Repeat the process several times until the brush is clean. Finally, comb the bristles with a steel comb and hang it by the handle so the bristles will dry straight. When the brush is dry, wrap it in foil or heavy

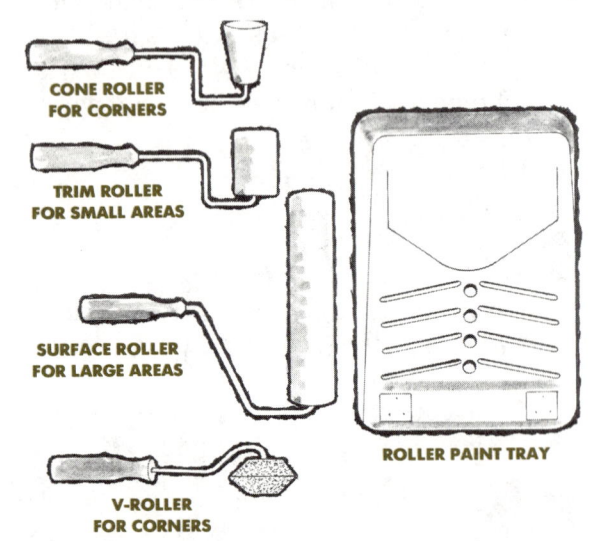

Figure 26-4: Rollers are available in almost as many shapes and sizes as brushes. Rollers are a fast method for painting large areas and are good on rough surfaces.

Figure 26-3: Wearing rubber gloves, work the solvent through the bristles with your fingers. Work from the handle out toward the ends of the bristles. When the brush is clean, comb the bristles straight with a metal comb. After it is dry, wrap it in foil or heavy paper and hang it up.

Painting Methods 73

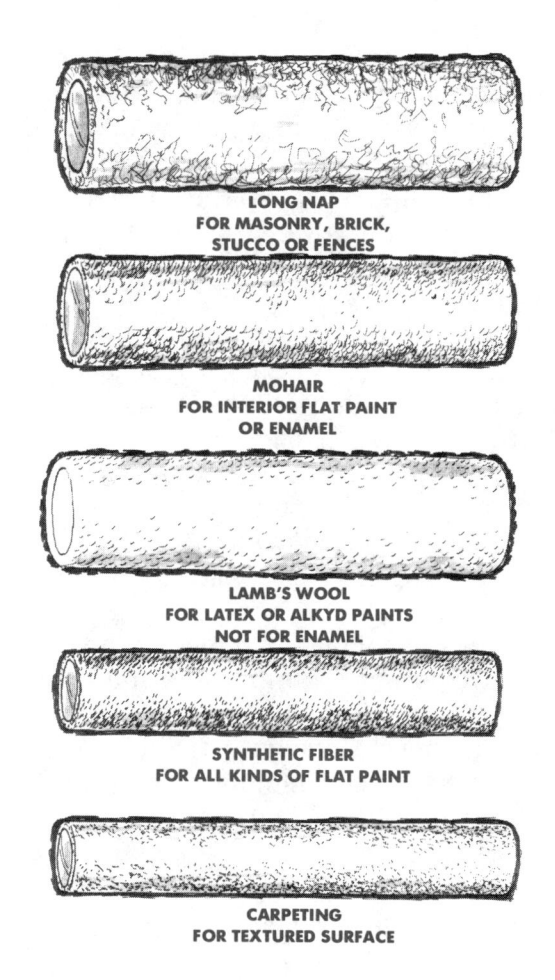

LONG NAP
FOR MASONRY, BRICK, STUCCO OR FENCES

MOHAIR
FOR INTERIOR FLAT PAINT OR ENAMEL

LAMB'S WOOL
FOR LATEX OR ALKYD PAINTS NOT FOR ENAMEL

SYNTHETIC FIBER
FOR ALL KINDS OF FLAT PAINT

CARPETING
FOR TEXTURED SURFACE

Figure 26-5: Rollers are made of different materials for different uses.

PAINT

ROLL OUT EXCESS

Figure 26-6: Do not fill the roller pan with paint. Leave enough room to roll out some of the excess paint from the roller.

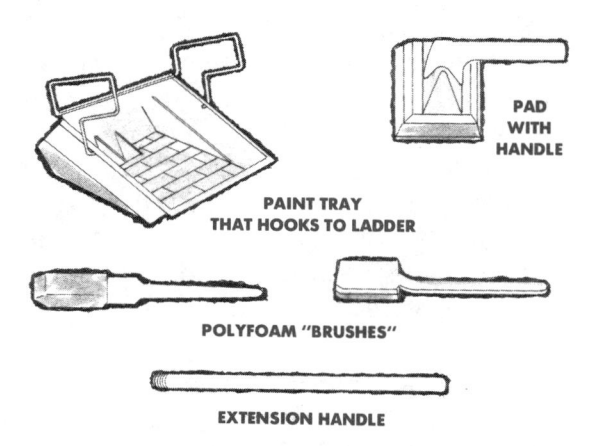

PAINT TRAY THAT HOOKS TO LADDER

PAD WITH HANDLE

POLYFOAM "BRUSHES"

EXTENSION HANDLE

Figure 26-7: Paint pads are made of the same materials as rollers. They also come in various shapes.

paper and hang it up by the handle. Never store a good brush without protecting the bristles.

Just like brushes, rollers also come in different shapes and sizes (figure 26-4). The roller should match the type of paint (figure 26-5).

If you get too much paint on a roller, it will splatter. So be sure you press out the excess paint in the roller pan (figure 26-6). Running the roller too fast will also make a mess. Dip the roller in paint, start in a spot a short distance from where you left off and work your way back. This will help prevent heavy spots and runs.

Some rollers are worth cleaning. Others are better used once and thrown away. Clean rollers in water or the proper solvent.

Painting pads also come in several shapes and sizes (figure 26-7). Many pads are made of the same material as rollers. The big difference is that the paint is wiped on instead of being rolled on. Clean paint from pads as you would clean rollers.

Spray painting equipment can be simple or complex. Bypass guns need a compressor but not an air tank. Other types need an air tank as well as a compressor. Some spray outfits have an electromagnetic vibrator in the gun and no hose or compressor. One type, called an airless sprayer, shoots a jet of pure paint without using any air at all. This type covers best and drifts least. Professionals use it for painting just about everything.

Always wear a mask when you spray paint. Experiment first. Test the gun before actually painting anything.

Keep the spray at right angles (90°) to the surface being painted. Start each stroke beyond the edge of the surface being painted, and move the gun with an even, parallel, back-and-forth stroke. Keep it moving so paint will not build up in one spot. Too much paint will ripple, blister, or run. Spray corners and edges first (figure 26-8).

If you must spray paint in a room, make certain it is ventilated well. Keep a fire extinguisher handy and wear a mask.

Clean spray equipment as soon as you finish. Spray the proper solvent through the gun before you take it apart. Use a tip cleaner or a broom straw to open clogged jets. A wire or nail will ruin the gun.

Spray cans are like small spray guns. A propellent gas forces paint through a spray nozzle.

Use a spray can as you would a spray gun. Never use a fanning motion. Hold the spray straight, 10 to 12 inches from the surface. Move it parallel to the surface and keep moving. If you stop for even a half second, you will get an orange-peel texture or the paint will run. Don't change direction until you've passed the edge of the job and are spraying into air.

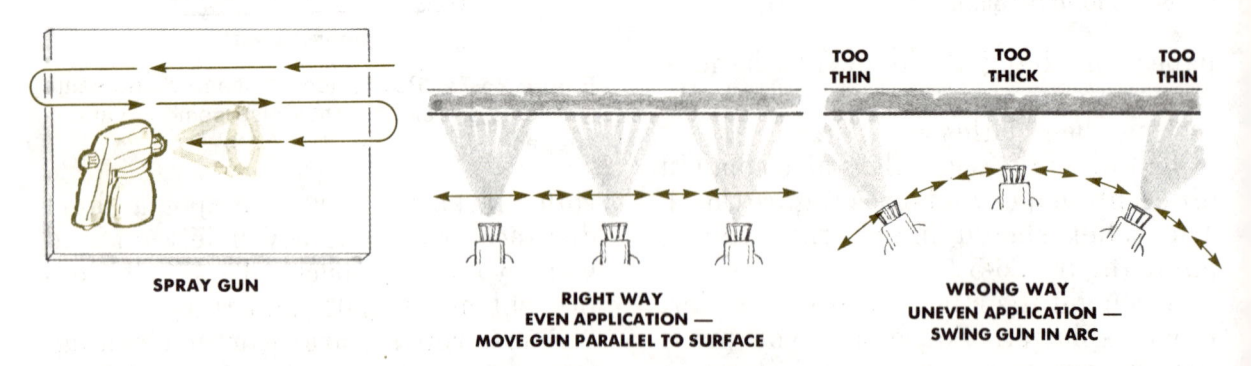

Figure 26-8: Using a spray gun well requires practice. The gun must be moved evenly, and kept at a constant distance from the surface being painted. Several light coats are always better than one heavy one.

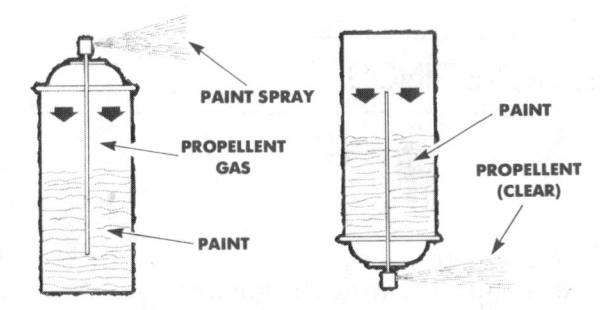

Figure 26-9: A compressed propellant forces paint out of the spray can in a fine mist. When you turn the can upside down and spray, the tube and nozzle are cleared.

Spray can paint is even thinner than paint used in spray guns. It doesn't cover as well and runs quicker. Two or three thin coats are better than one heavy coat. Give the paint plenty of time to dry between coats. While you're waiting, turn the spray can upside down and spray until clear air comes out of the nozzle (figure 26-9).

This cleans the nozzle so the paint won't dry and clog it before you want to spray the next coat.

Because spray cans are under great pressure, they can explode, and careless handling can be dangerous. They should never be punctured or thrown into a fire. Store them in a cool place, away from hot water and heating pipes.

SELF CHECK

1. What is the traditional way to paint?
2. Are all paint rollers the same?
3. What are paint pads?
4. How do you hold a spray gun or spray can to paint evenly?

Unit 27 WALL COVERINGS

Not too long ago, the only wall covering available was wallpaper. Today wall coverings are made of many materials other than paper. Fabric and vinyl are good examples. Some types are prepasted or have adhesive on the back. No matter which type you use, the basic procedures are the same. You will have to:

- Measure
- Prepare the wall surface
- Prepare and hang wall covering

To find out how much wall area must be covered, measure each wall and multiply its width by its height. Adding the answers will give you the total area of the wall surface (figure 27-1). Next measure the doors and windows. Find

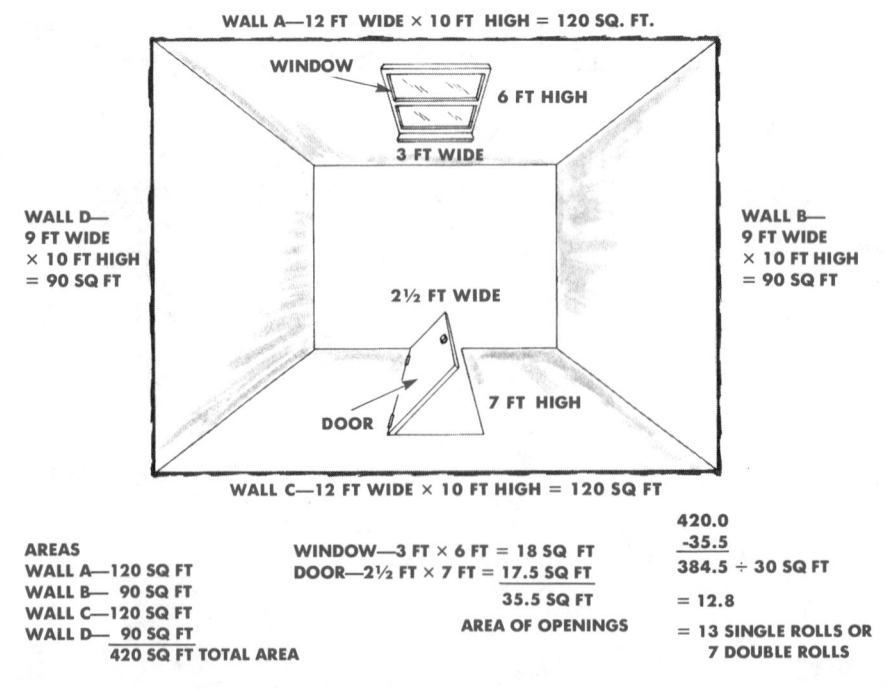

WALL A—12 FT WIDE × 10 FT HIGH = 120 SQ. FT.

WINDOW — 6 FT HIGH, 3 FT WIDE

WALL D— 9 FT WIDE × 10 FT HIGH = 90 SQ FT

WALL B— 9 FT WIDE × 10 FT HIGH = 90 SQ FT

DOOR — 2½ FT WIDE, 7 FT HIGH

WALL C—12 FT WIDE × 10 FT HIGH = 120 SQ FT

```
AREAS                    WINDOW—3 FT × 6 FT = 18 SQ FT        420.0
WALL A—120 SQ FT         DOOR—2½ FT × 7 FT = 17.5 SQ FT       -35.5
WALL B— 90 SQ FT                             35.5 SQ FT       384.5 ÷ 30 SQ FT
WALL C—120 SQ FT                         AREA OF OPENINGS     = 12.8
WALL D— 90 SQ FT                                              = 13 SINGLE ROLLS OR
       420 SQ FT TOTAL AREA                                     7 DOUBLE ROLLS
```

Figure 27-1: To figure the amount of wall covering needed, calculate the area of all walls to be covered (minus window and door openings) and divide by 30 (the number of square feet per roll).

Wall Coverings

their total area by multiplying each one's height by width and adding them together. Now subtract the total area of the openings from the total area of the wall surface. The answer is the wall area to be covered. Since one roll of wallcovering contains about 30 square feet, divide this number by 30. The answer is the number of rolls you will need.

Many do-it-yourself wallpapering kits contain all the tools you will need. Some of the basic tools are shown in figure 27-2.

Before you begin, the wall surface should be clean and free from loose plaster and paper. Surfaces painted with enamel should be sanded to remove the gloss and assure good adhesion. Remove any old wallpaper. Use a steamer (figure 27-3) or wallpaper remover to lift the paper, and then strip it off. (Caution: wallpaper remover is caustic—follow directions and wear rubber gloves.)

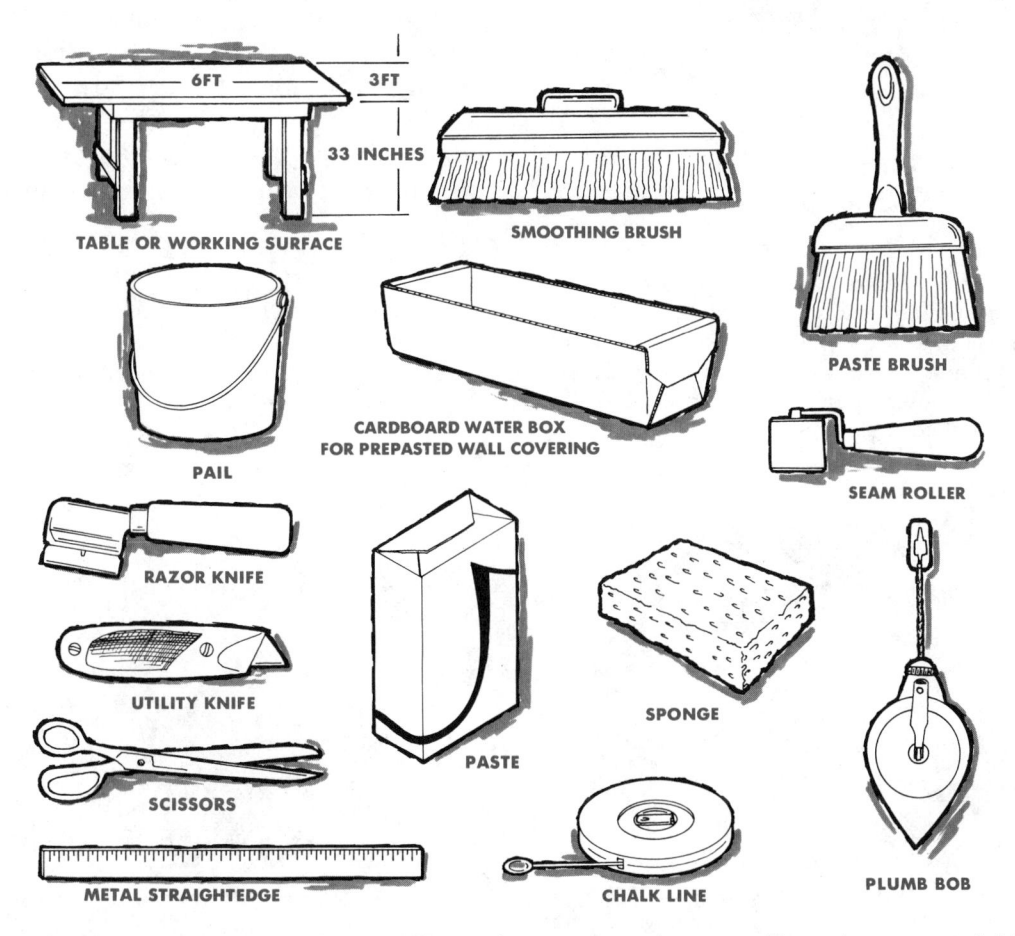

Figure 27-2: Depending on the type of wall covering you are using, you will need some special tools to apply the covering properly.

New walls must be primed before covering.

The most difficult job is hanging the wall covering just right. Begin by attaching a plumb bob to the end of a chalk line. Measure the width of one roll (usually 23½ inches) from the starting point and hang the plumb bob. Snap the chalk line on the wall. This line will serve as a guide for hanging the first piece.

Figure 27-3: If the old wallpaper is loose, if you are going to hang vinyl wall covering, or if there are several layers of wallpaper on your wall already, it is best to remove all the old paper before you hang the new paper. This can be done most easily by renting a steamer.

Figure 27-4: Apply paste to the bottom two-thirds of the sheet and fold up carefully. Do not crease. Finish applying the paste and carry the folded sheet to the wall.

Cover your table or work surface with several layers of newspaper and unroll the first strip of wall covering. Cut the first piece, allowing two inches of overlap at the ceiling and two inches at the floor. Unroll the next piece and place it alongside the first to match the pattern. Cut enough strips to cover one wall and number them on the back.

Spread paste on the back of the first strip. Be sure to leave no dry spots and pay special attention to the edges. Loosely fold up the bottom half, printed side out, for ease in carrying (figure 27-4). Position the strip at the ceiling and smooth it with a brush, working from the center out to the edges (figure 27-5). Unfold the bottom section and continue smoothing down.

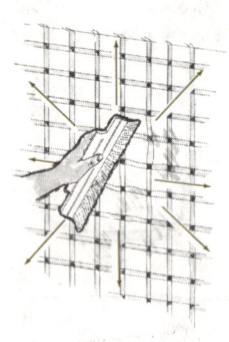

Figure 27-5: Brush wallpaper from the center out to the edges. Smooth out all air bubbles.

Figure 27-6: Trim overlap with a straight, even line.

Be sure to work out all of the air bubbles. After about 15 minutes the top and bottom overlap can be trimmed with a sharp blade (figure 27-6). To prevent getting paste on the next strip, remove the top layer of newspaper from the table before you apply paste to the next strip.

Other types of wall coverings may need to be soaked in water or the paste may have to be applied directly to the wall. Follow the manufacturer's instructions or ask the person who sells the wall covering.

Two types of seams can be used to join wall coverings (figure 27-7). The overlap joint is one in which the sheets actually overlap each other. When using overlapped joints, begin alongside a window and work away from it. This will make the joints less conspicuous. Butt joints are preferred by professionals. The edge of each strip runs along the edge of the previous strip without overlapping. When using butt joints, begin hanging paper on the longest wall space without windows or doors and work around the room. For either type of seam, wait about 15 minutes for the paste to set and then press down with a seam roller (figure 27-8). Carefully trim around electrical boxes.

Much valuable information is often printed in the margins of the wall covering, including trim marks, marks to help you match the pattern, mill run number and manufacturer. Be sure to buy enough wall covering at the start because you may have difficulty matching colors or patterns later.

Figure 27-8: After the paper has been hanging for about 15 minutes, roll over the seams with a seam roller.

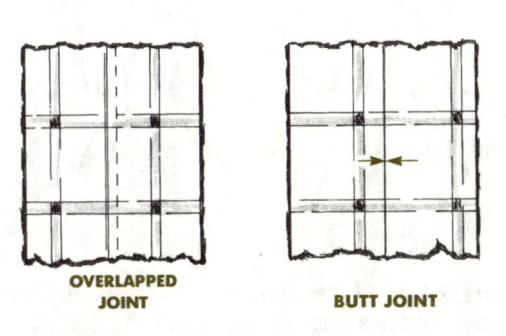

Figure 27-7: Wall covering joints are either overlapped or butt joints. Professionals prefer butt joints.

SELF CHECK

1. How do you determine the amount of wall covering needed for a room?
2. What tools are necessary to hang wall coverings?
3. What is the most difficult part of hanging wall coverings?
4. What types of joints can be used for wall coverings?

Unit 28   PANELING AND TRIM

There are many ways to improve the appearance and value of a home. With the widespread use of drywall two of the most common improvements are:
- Wall trim
- Paneling

Wall trim includes molding and baseboards. Molding comes in various styles (figure 28-1) and covers the places where wall and floor and where wall and ceiling meet. It is used to cover the rough edges at the ceiling and floor when walls are paneled. Molding may also cover joints or nails where paneling meets.

Baseboards are high moldings that run along the wall at floor level. They

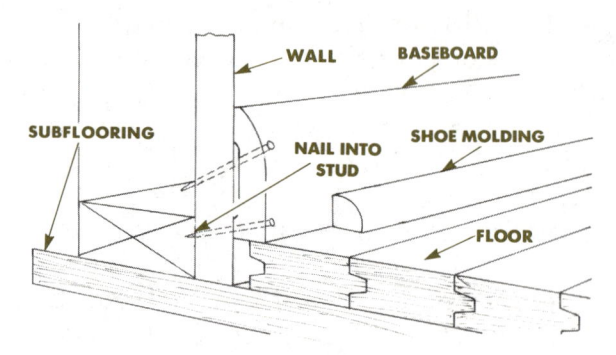

Figure 28-2: Baseboards are a type of molding that run along the bottom of a wall next to the floor. They protect the walls and are not difficult to remove or replace.

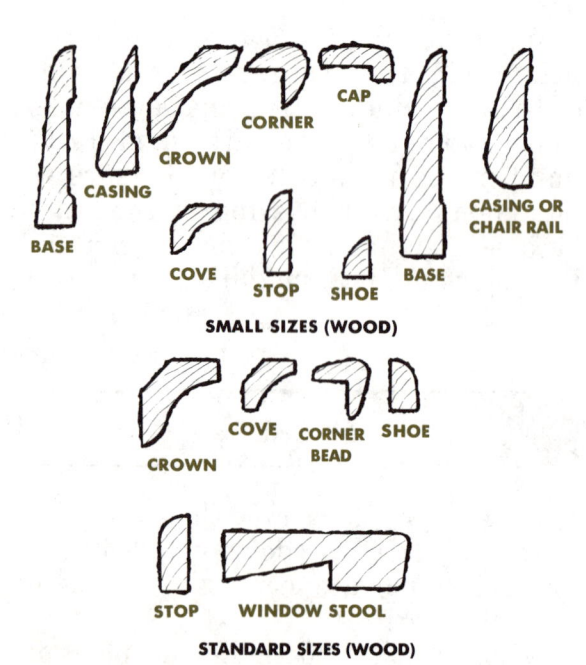

Figure 28-1: Wood trim is used around the ceiling and around the floor especially where wall paneling has been installed.

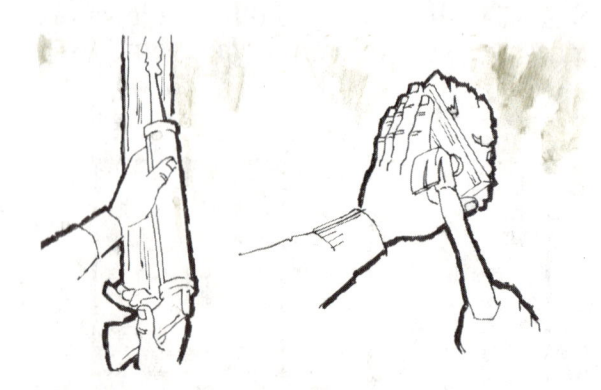

Figure 28-3: Adhesives for gluing panels come in tubes and are applied with a calking gun. Move a cloth-covered block over the face of the panel while striking the block with a mallet. This spreads the glue.

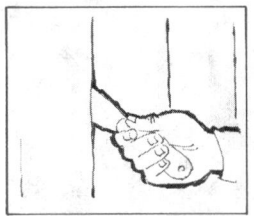

| FORCE PUTTY KNIFE BETWEEN PANEL AND STUD | WORK PRY BAR IN TO BREAK GLUE LOOSE | PULL BRADS OR DRIVE THEM THROUGH | IF YOU CAN'T GET THE PANEL OFF IN ONE PIECE, SPLIT IT DOWN ONE EDGE AND SAVE AS MUCH AS YOU CAN TO USE ELSEWHERE |

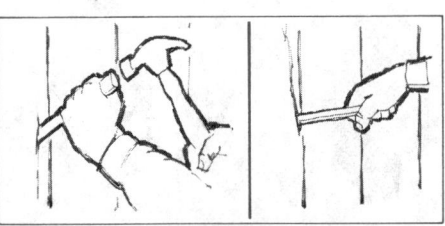

Figure 28-4: Glued panels seldom come off in one piece. Pry them off and save the pieces to make a pattern for the replacement panel.

are often damaged by vacuum cleaners, shoes, toys, and similar objects. Baseboards are usually nailed down lightly so they can be easily removed or replaced (figure 28-2).

Paneling comes in 4' x 8' sheets and is made of wood, plastic, rock, cork, or some other material. Several years ago paneling was nailed in place. Today much of the new paneling is glued.

Sometimes a panel will come loose. If the loose part is over a stud or joist, it can be nailed down with a colored finishing nail. When the loose section is not over a stud or joist, panel cement can be forced behind the loose panel. Pound the area with a mallet and padded block while the glue is drying to push it tightly against the wall (figure 28-3).

The best way to repair a damaged panel is to replace the entire panel. This may be difficult to do if the panel has been glued and nailed. First carefully remove the molding and baseboard. Then use a thin chisel to pry a corner of the panel loose in order to break the panel free from the glue (figure 28-4). Use the old piece as a pattern for cutting the new piece. Remove old glue from the studs or drywall. Apply new panel cement and press the new panel into place. Pound the panel with a mallet and padded block. Drive several small nails into the panel to hold it down while the glue dries. Afterwards, set the nails with a nail set and cover the holes with a putty stick. Large pieces of old paneling may be kept for patchwork.

SELF CHECK

1. What is molding used for?
2. What are baseboards?
3. How should loose paneling be fastened down?
4. How would you replace a damaged piece of paneling?

5 STRUCTURAL MAINTENANCE

Modern buildings need continual upkeep and repair. Roofs must withstand harsh weather and keep the inside of the house dry. Doors and windows are subject to frequent use, and they wear out or break. If not kept in good repair, these things can become a nuisance or a more serious problem.

This section will explain how to replace a broken pane of glass and how to keep doors and windows operating smoothly. You will also learn some ways to keep your roof in good shape. A little maintenance can often save you a big and costly repair job later on.

FLOOR COVERINGS   Unit 29

Hardwood floors are usually oak or maple. Softwood floors, usually made of pine, wear better when they are covered with
- Rugs or Carpets
- Linoleum
- Tile

Carpeting is fastened down professionally. A damaged section can be cut out and a new patch sewn, glued, tacked, taped or stapled in place (figure 29-1).

Today linoleum is made of vinyl. It is thinner and softer but more durable than the original oil cloth linoleum. If water seeps under linoleum, the edges will come loose and begin to curl. Dry out the area and work cement under the loose edges. Pile on sandbags. Some excess cement will ooze out. Clean it up before it dries.

To lay a patch, cut the new piece the exact size of the hole. Match the pattern and cut the piece with a slight

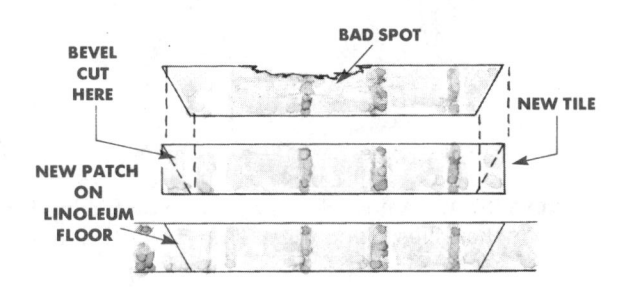

Figure 29-2: Linoleum patches can be set in. Be careful to match the pattern. Cutting a beveled edge helps keep the patch in place and makes the cut line less noticeable.

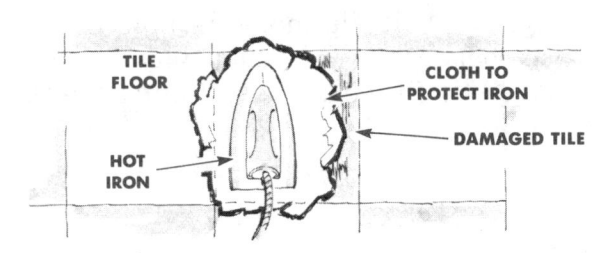

Figure 29-3: Tiles are easy to remove when you heat them with a pressing iron.

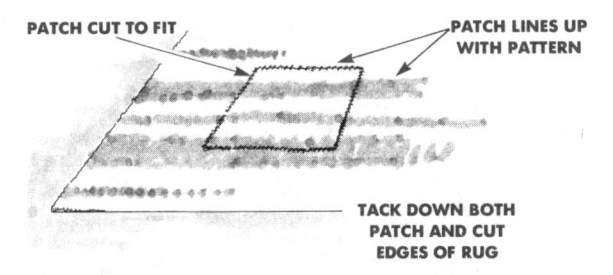

Figure 29-1: A damaged piece of carpet can be cut out and replaced. The patch and rug must be fastened down.

bevel (figure 29-2). Remove all of the old cement or the patch will bulge. Set in the new piece and hold it down with sandbags.

Vinyl and asphalt are the materials most often used for floor tiles. Vinyl is soft and pliable. Asphalt tile is thicker, harder, and tends to chip. Remove a damaged tile by heating it with a hot pressing iron over a cloth (figure 29-3). Scrape up all the old cement while it is warm and soft.

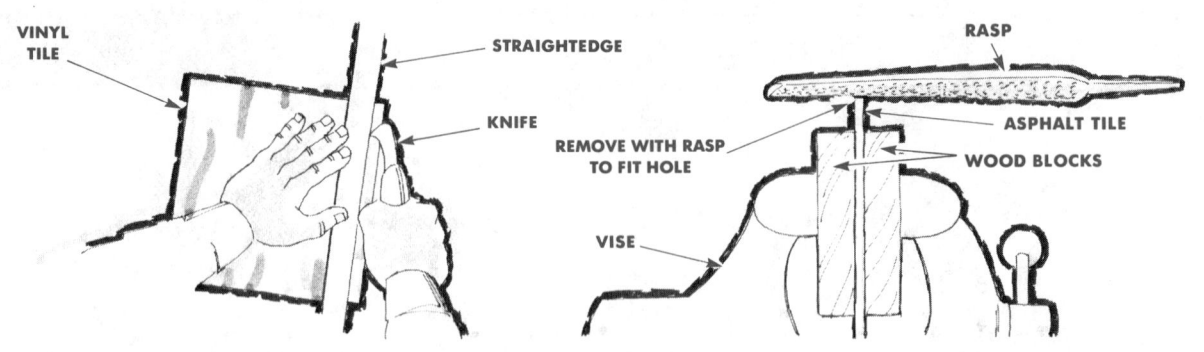

Figure 29-4: A new tile may have to be trimmed to fit. Trim vinyl tiles with a knife and straightedge. To trim asphalt tiles place them in a vise between wood blocks and file them down with a rasp.

You may have to trim the new tile. Use a knife and straightedge to trim vinyl. Asphalt tile should be placed in a vise between two wood blocks and shaved down with a rasp (figure 29-4).

SELF CHECK

1. What is the difference between linoleum and vinyl?
2. How should you cut a linoleum patch?
3. How is a damaged floor tile removed?
4. How would you trim an asphalt tile?

WINDOW FRAMES   Unit 30

Many window frames are made of wood (figure 30-1). The most common problem with window frames is sticking caused by:
- Paint
- Swelling
- Warping
- Broken sash cords

New paint is a major cause of windows sticking. Sticking of freshly painted windows can be prevented by leaving the window slightly open while painting. As soon as the paint dries, slide the window up and down. Do not wait too long because paint hardens as it ages.

If the window has been painted shut for a while, it will be difficult to open. Use a putty knife to cut through the paint seal (figure 30-2). Never pry the window open with a chisel or pry bar.

Figure 30-2: Painting across the moving parts of a window is a major cause of sticking. Running a putty knife between the stop and the sash will help free the window.

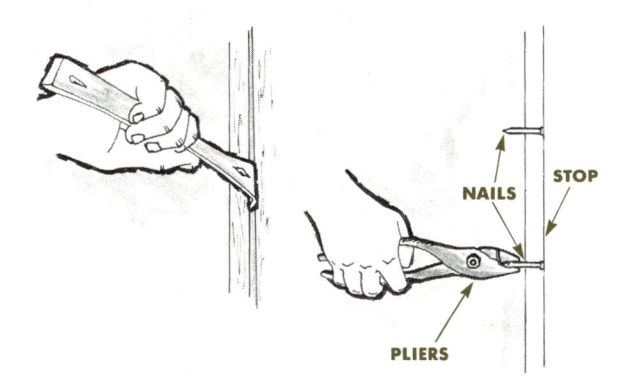

Figure 30-3: Remove the window only as a last resort. Carefully remove the stops, then pull the nails out through the back of the stop with pliers.

Even if you use a piece of wood to protect the sill, the window sash will be dented.

Windows that are badly stuck may have to be removed from the frame. The sliding part of the window (sash) is held in place by two strips of wood called stops. Carefully pry up the stops (figure 30-3). Remember, you want to

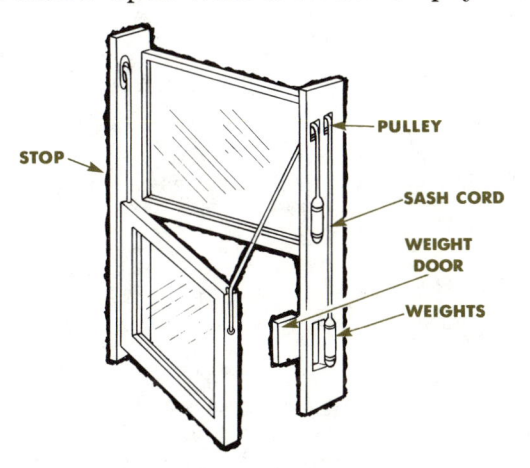

Figure 30-1: Most older houses have wooden window frames. However, most new homes have plastic or aluminum frames.

85

use these stops again. A little patience saves buying, cutting, fitting, and painting a new piece of wood. Don't drive the nails back out through the stop after the stop is off. Use pliers and pull the nails out through the back side of the stop. This will leave a neat little hole.

With the sash out, you may sand or scrape off the excess paint. When the weather is dry, cover any bare wood with a thin coat of paint or fast-drying sealer.

Paint protects wood frames. If moisture soaks the frame, the wood will swell. Never plane a frame that is swollen. Otherwise, when the wood dries, it will be too loose and will rattle in the wind. Instead, rub paraffin, soap, or a stick lubricant on the frame (figure 30-4). Warped frames should be planed or sanded. If the wood is warped too much, it must be replaced.

If a sash cord breaks or the weight comes loose, the window will hang crooked, and the window won't stay up. To fix the cord, pry off the stops. Find the sash weight door and remove it. Usually it is held in place by one or two screws. Reach inside and take out the weight (figure 30-5). If the sash cord is still good, the weight probably came untied. Retie it and put everything back together.

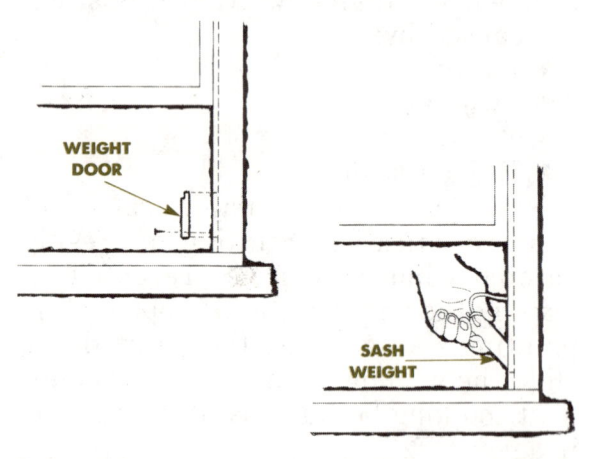

Figure 30-5: To repair a sash cord, remove the door in the window frame, reach in, and take out the sash weight.

Figure 30-4: Lubricate all moving surfaces on the window and frame with a hard piece of soap or paraffin to help them slide better.

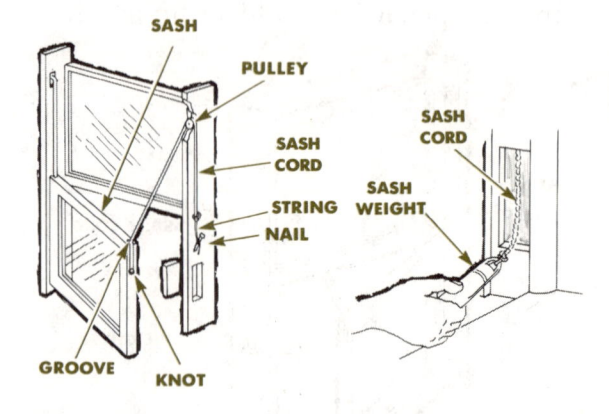

Figure 30-6: Tie a knot in one end of the sash cord and fit it into the sash groove. Tie a nail to the other end for weight and feed the cord over the pulley. Raise the window and reach into the opening. Pull out the new cord. Tie it to the sash weight.

If you need a new sash cord, make sure it's the same thickness as the old one or it won't run through the pulley. Feed the new cord through and tie one end to the sash and the other end to the weight (figure 30-6). The sash cord will stretch, so leave some room under the weight so it won't hit bottom later and keep the window from opening all the way. Move the window up and down to see if you've tied the weight too high or too low. When you're sure everything works, put it back together again.

When you put the stops back, ignore the old nail holes. Tap the nails in a new place, but, to avoid hammer dents, stop before you hit the frame. Finish driving the nails with a nail set. Cover the nail heads and fill in the old holes with wood putty. After several days, when the putty is dry, touch up with paint.

As a building ages, it settles. Structural settling is another cause for windows jamming. If the windows are being twisted out of line, the entire frame must be removed and reset in the wall.

Wood frame windows are often replaced by aluminum ones. Other new frames are vinyl (plastic) over a wood core.

Casement windows open with a crank that needs a yearly greasing (figure 30-7). Because these cranks rust, you will have to keep them clean and painted. Casement windows are usually easier to care for than wooden frame windows.

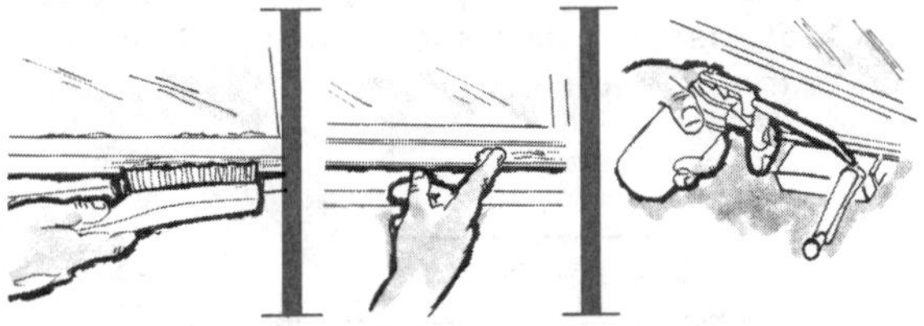

Figure 30-7: Clean casement window cranks at least once a year. Grease the track and oil the crank handle and window hinges.

SELF CHECK

1. How does paint cause windows to stick?
2. Why shouldn't you plane swollen wood frames?
3. How should you remove the stops on a wood frame window?
4. How should window stops be replaced?

Unit 31 GLAZING

When working with glass, pay attention to what you are doing and be careful. Wear safety glasses when breaking scored glass. Clean up all debris, broken glass, and glass splinters immediately.

Cutting and fitting glass is called glazing. Glazing is actually done in three steps:
- Measuring the frame
- Cutting the glass
- Installing the glass

Begin by removing the old glass. Wear heavy work gloves. Spread some newspaper on the floor to catch small pieces of broken glass. Remove all old glass, putty, glazier's points, and old paint from the frame. Sand the frame if it is wood or paint it if it is metal.

Measuring is the most important step in replacing a pane of glass. If the piece is cut too small, the glass will fall out of the frame. You cannot trim less than 3/16 inch from a piece of glass that is just a little too big. Measure twice, cut once is a good rule.

Start by measuring exactly the inside of the frame into which the glass will fit. Then subtract 1/8 inch from each measurement (length and width), figure 31-1. This allows for irregularities in the frame or glass. Lightly mark the edge of the glass with a three-corner file (figure 31-2).

Place the glass on a flat table or special cutting board. If the table isn't flat, first cover it with several layers of

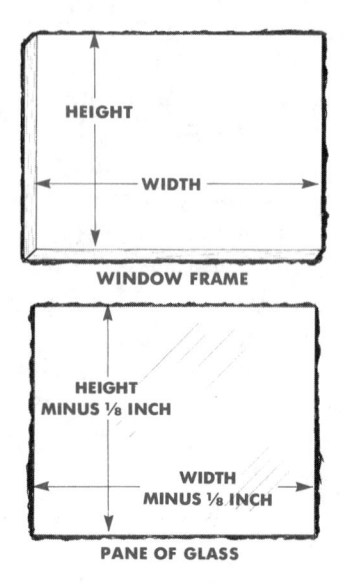

Figure 31-1: When replacing a piece of glass, cut the glass 1/8 inch shorter and 1/8 inch narrower than the frame.

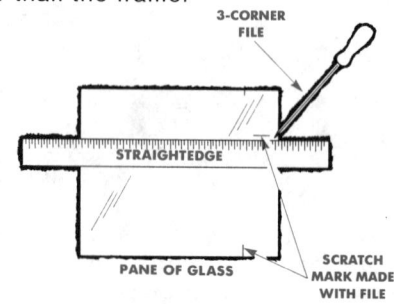

Figure 31-2: Use a three-cornered file to mark the dimensions on the glass.

soft cloth. Use a T-square or straightedge to make the cut. Allow for the distance from the edge of the cutter to the center of the cutting wheel (figure 31-3). Kerosene along the cut line will prevent the glass from splintering.

Glazing 89

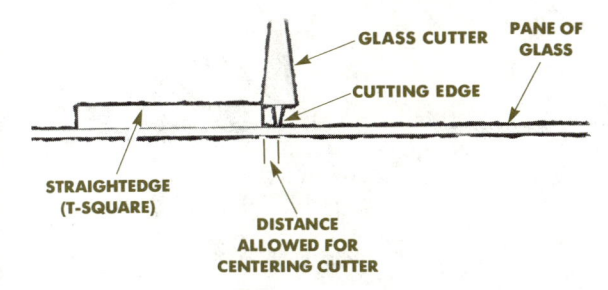

Figure 31-3: Line up a T-square or ruler. Then move it over slightly so the center of the cutter wheel runs along the marked line.

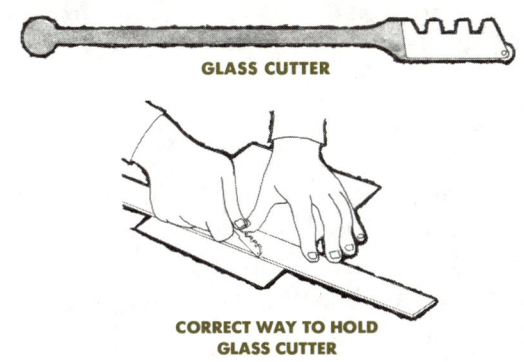

Figure 31-4: Press down hard enough for the cutter to dig into the glass. Once you start moving the cutter, don't stop until the cut is finished. Use kerosene to lubricate the cutter and prevent the glass from splintering.

Figure 31-5: After the glass is scored, slide it to the edge of the table and tap on the bottom side while bending gently. The sooner you break the glass after scoring, the easier it is. In a day or two the glass "forgets" the scored line and will crack anywhere.

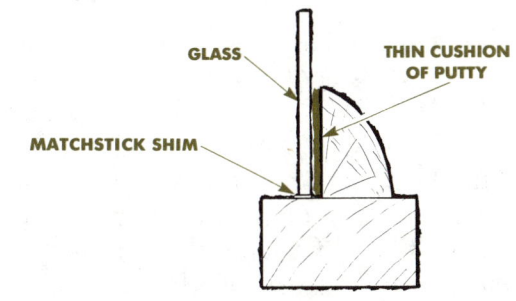

Figure 31-6: Spread putty over the frame and press the glass into place. Then insert glazier's points and cover with putty.

Score the glass with the cutter (figure 31-4). Then slide the glass over to the edge of the table and tap gently on the bottom side while bending gently (figure 31-5). This should be done right after glass is scored! Otherwise the glass should be scored again just before it is finally cut.

Install the cut glass in a wood frame window with glazier's points and putty. Glazier's putty or glazing compound dries hard. The putty used on wood frames can be softened with linseed oil. If you've used too much oil, remove some by rolling the putty on newspaper.

First spread a thin layer of glazier's putty inside the frame. Place the glass and press firmly into the putty. Small pieces of wood, called shims, can be inserted below the glass to center it (figure 31-6).

Press glazier's points into the wood along each edge of the glass. Only a few points are needed because the glass is held in place by the hardened putty, not the glazier's points. Do not use a

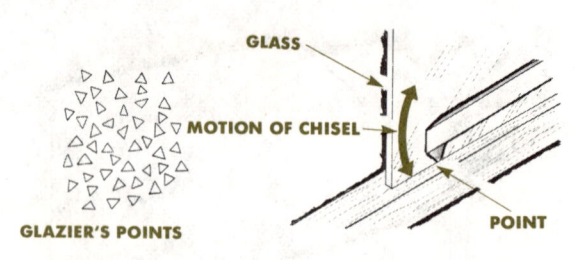

Figure 31-7: Glazier's points are usually set by pressing them into place with a chisel or screwdriver.

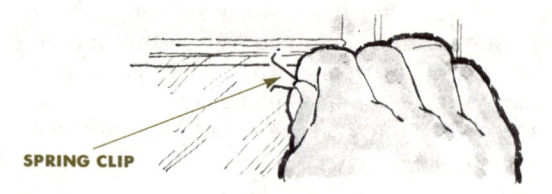

Figure 31-8: Metal frame windows use spring clips in place of glazier's points.

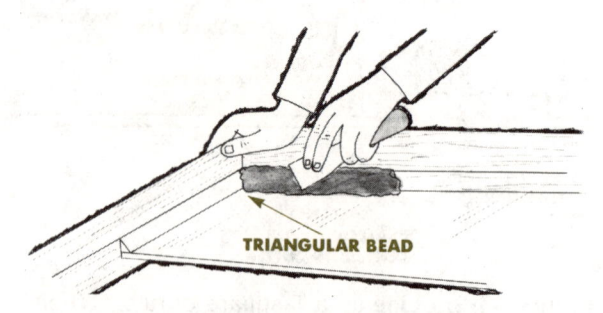

Figure 31-9: Linseed oil is used to soften putty. Excess oil is rolled out on newspaper. Then the putty is pressed down and the excess removed with a putty knife.

hammer to set the points. Press them into place with a chisel or piece of wood (figure 31-7). Casement windows use spring clips instead of glazier's points. Place the clips into the holes provided (figure 31-8).

Take more putty and roll it into a rope about 1/4-inch thick. Press it into the joint between the glass and frame. Then finish by smoothing and removing the excess putty with a putty knife (figure 31-9).

Glazier's putty takes a week to harden completely. After that it may be painted. You can scrape off paint smears on the glass with a single-edge razor blade. But it is easy to mask the glass with newspaper and tape before painting.

SELF CHECK

1. What are some of the precautions you should take when handling glass?
2. What are the three steps in a glazing job?
3. Why should kerosene be smeared on glass before cutting?
4. What kind of putty is used to frame glass?

DOORS AND FRAMES — Unit 32

Doors are subject to constant use, so it is understandable that they don't always open and close properly. All doors have the same problems. They are caused either by the frame and door or by the hardware. Door and frame problems include:
- Swelling
- Warping
- A loose fit

Wood swells when moisture gets into it. Never sand or plane a swollen door. Wait until the weather gets drier or remove the door and keep it in a dry, warm place until the swelling goes down. If the door continues to stick even after the wood is dry, inspect it to find out where it is binding. Then lightly sand the area until the door moves freely. Seal the wood and finish with paint or varnish. The sealer and paint will keep moisture from swelling the wood again. Be sure to seal top and bottom of doors as well.

Humidity can also cause doors to warp. A warped door lets heat out in the winter and, in summer, lets heat in. You can straighten a warped door by removing the door and piling weights on the bulging part. But it's usually easier to pry loose the side stop and renail it to fit the warped door (figure 32-1).

Since there is always a little swelling and shrinking, doors should be slightly smaller than their openings. To have the door work properly but fit tightly, use weather stripping. The simplest weather stripping is adhesive-backed plastic foam. To install it, first clean the door stop. Remove grease and dirt. Then press the weather stripping along the top and side of the door frame (figure 32-2).

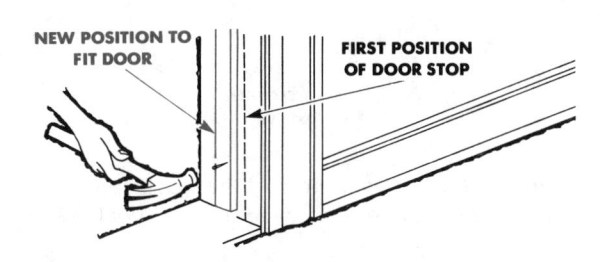

Figure 32-1: Since straightened doors frequently warp again, it is easier to move the door stop to fit the door than to try to reshape the door. Remove the stop. With the door closed, draw a guide line on the frame and renail the stop along this line.

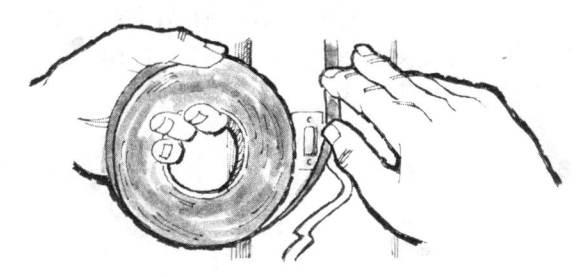

Figure 32-2: Self-adhesive weather stripping is pressed along the door stop as the paper backing is removed.

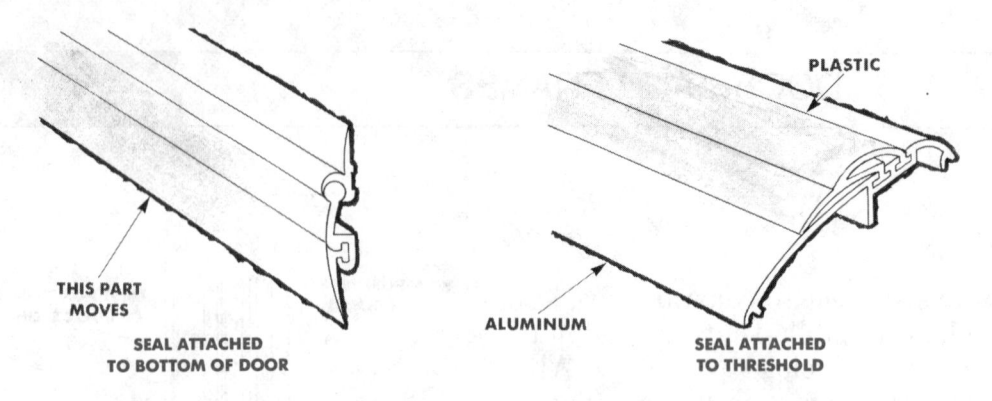

Figure 32-3: The bottom of the door can be sealed with a special strip attached directly to the door. Another type of seal, made of plastic and aluminum, fits right into the threshold.

Seal the bottom of the door with a folding (hinged) threshold seal, or use a special aluminum-plastic strip that tacks into the threshold (figure 32-3). You can purchase weather stripping in specific lengths or cut it to size.

SELF CHECK

1. What is the best way to prevent wood from swelling?
2. What is the best way to fix a warped door?
3. How is weather stripping applied?
4. How can you keep drafts from coming in below the door?

DOOR HARDWARE Unit 33

Door problems are often caused by the door and frame. But hardware can also be the cause of doors sticking. <u>Hardware</u> refers to the metal parts on a door:
- Hinges
- Faceplates and latches
- Strike plates

In time, hinges loosen up and let the door sag so it no longer fits the frame (figure 33-1). This happens when the screws pull loose. The cure is to remove the loose screw or screws. Fill the hole with wood putty or with a wooden matchstick or soft wood plug covered with white glue (figure 33-2). Without drilling a hole, replace the screw in the plugged hole.

It is much easier to rehang a hinge than to rebuild a door frame. Often a cardboard shim behind one of the hinges (figure 33-3) will shift the door enough to prevent binding. Sometimes removing one hinge and chiseling the mortise a little deeper (figure 33-4) will correct both top and side clearances.

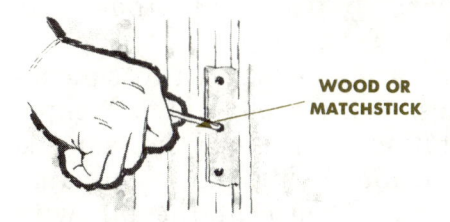

Figure 33-2: By plugging a loose screw hole with wood putty or soft wood like a matchstick, you can reset the screw. Sometimes you will need a longer screw as well.

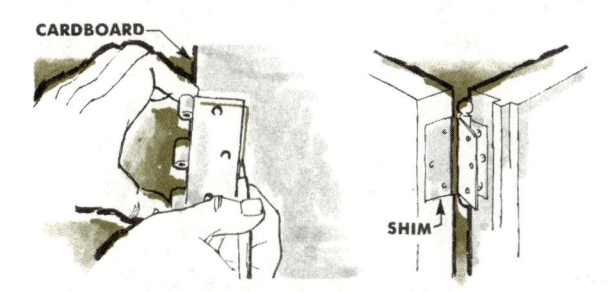

Figure 33-3: Cut a piece of cardboard to place behind the side of the hinge that looks strongest. If two or more shims are needed, place them behind both sides of the hinge. If a door is sticking at the top, shim the top edge. If it is binding at the bottom, shim the bottom hinge.

Figure 33-1: Loose hinges are a frequent cause of tilting doors that don't fit their frames.

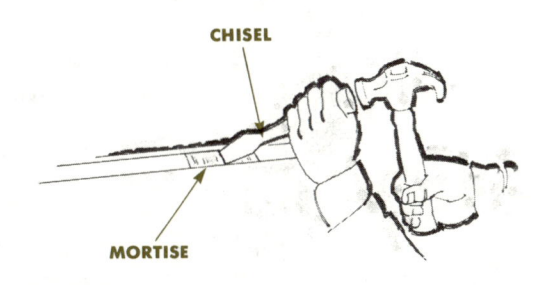

Figure 33-4: Another way to repair a door is by setting the hinge deeper into the wooden frame. This is called mortising.

To work on the hinges, remove the bottom pivot pin first (figure 33-5). If you remove the top pin first, the weight of the door may tear the bottom hinge loose.

Squeaking doors are really squeaking hinges. Oil is really only a temporary solution. To stop the squeak, remove the hinge pivot pin. Sandpaper off any rust. Then coat the pin with paraffin, graphite lubricant, or silicon spray and replace it. Never use oil; it collects dust and becomes sticky.

Latches and faceplates also cause problems (figure 33-6). If the screws holding them to the door are loose, the door won't close properly. Reset the screws after plugging the original holes with wooden matchsticks or soft wood just as you did the hinge screws.

Strike plates on the door frame (figure 33-7) can also be a problem. When a door frame sags, the latch in the door may travel across the strike plate without meeting the hole in the strike plate. Remove the strike plate and place it in a vise. With a file enlarge the hole enough to accommodate the latch. If there is a bolt hole, enlarge it also. Before you replace the strike plate, chisel out the wood behind the enlarged hole.

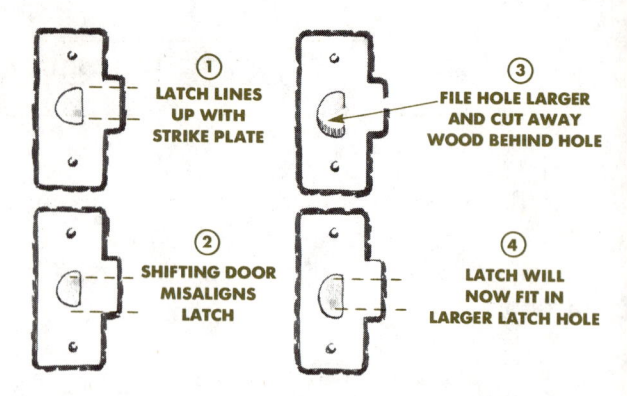

Figure 33-7: Strike plates should not be moved. It is better to enlarge the hole so the latch will meet.

Figure 33-5: The hinge pin holds the two parts of the hinge together and lets the door swing. To remove the pin, tap it with a hammer and screwdriver. Always remove the bottom pin first.

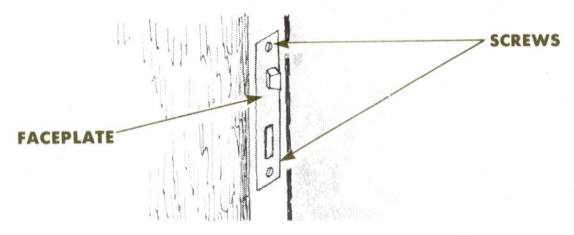

Figure 33-6: The faceplate surrounds the latch on the door. Be sure the screws that hold it on are tightly in place.

SELF CHECK

1. What hardware is usually found on a door?
2. How do you repair a loose door hinge?
3. How would you take down a door?
4. What is the best way to fix a door that won't latch?

ROOFS   Unit 34

One of the worst things that can happen to a house is a leaking roof. Once water gets in, it ruins ceilings and walls and can short electrical wiring. To repair a leaking roof you must:
- Find the leak
- Repair it with the proper roofing material

Working on a roof is always dangerous. It is possible to fall through or off even a flat roof. Roofs are not as solid as they seem. Test the roof before putting your weight on your foot. Try to step on rafters. If you are working in one area, use a large sheet of 1/2″ plywood to spread your weight across the rafters. On a steep roof, a ladder with a hook on one end can provide a safe footing (figure 34-1). Tie yourself to a safety line looped around a chimney or vent pipe. Make repairs only in good weather when there is little or no wind.

The first sign of a leak is usually a wet spot or dripping water in the house. A leak can be difficult to find. If the wet spot would always appear under the leak, the solution would be simple. When rain water comes through the roof, it often travels some distance before it becomes visible (figure 34-2).

Figure 34-1: Build a ladder hook to give yourself a safe place to stand while repairing a roof. A skyhook accessory is for working on gutters and windows but it can also be used to secure a ladder over most roof peaks. Never lean a ladder against gutters.

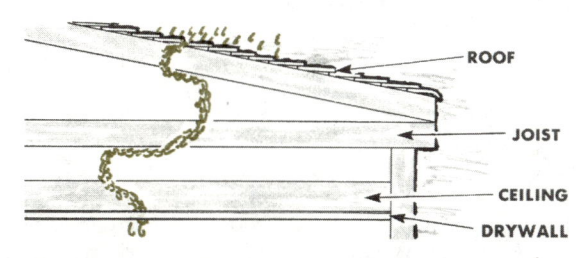

Figure 34-2: Roof leaks are not so easy to find. Try to trace them on a rainy day or have someone water your roof with a garden hose while you look for the leak.

Figure 34-3: When you find a leak in the attic, push a finishing nail or a piece of wire through. Don't use a nail with a large head because you'll want to pull it on through once you've marked the spot on the outside.

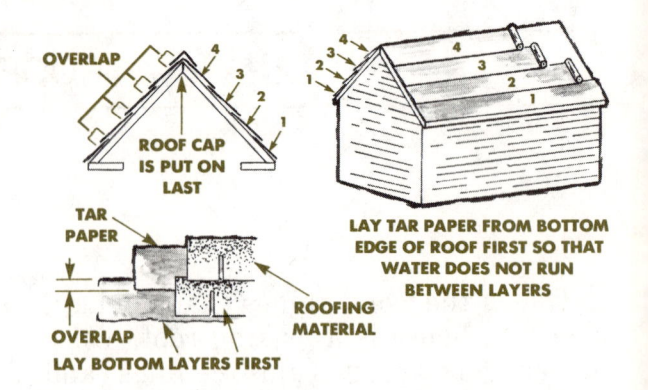

Figure 34-4: On slanted roofs, all roofing materials overlap. Gravity helps keep water from getting into the house.

Check the roof from the inside and try to trace the path of water back to the source. If that doesn't work, look for a pinpoint of light coming through the roof on a sunny day. If you find the hole, push a long finishing nail through so it can be seen outside (figure 34-3).

You can make small temporary repairs with asphalt roof cement. More permanent repairs are made by replacing a section of roofing material.

Flat roofs are often covered with tar paper and sealed with hot-mopped asphalt. Leaks can be sealed by applying more asphalt.

In general, roofing comes in four forms:
- Rolls
- Sheets
- Shingles
- Tiles

Roll roofing is usually layers of tar paper and layers of roofing material that overlap each former layer by at least four inches (figure 34-4). New roofing is usually laid right over the old.

Metal roofs, lead, copper, tin, or aluminum, usually come in sheets or rolls. Copper will change color but will never rust and will last practically forever. Tin roofs are actually made of iron that has been coated with lead (terne plate) or zinc (galvanized). Tin roofs will rust unless they are painted. Aluminum will not corrode unless it is near the ocean. To repair metal roofs, you can solder patches on copper or tin. Solder will not hold on aluminum so you should use asphalt roof cement and nail patches with special nails. Cover each nail with an asphalt emulsion to prevent leaks.

All shingles were once made of wood. Now composition and asphalt shingles are quite popular. Cement down any loose shingles. Replace those that are badly damaged. Lift the bad shingle carefully and run a hacksaw blade under it to cut off the nails holding it in place (figure 34-5). If needed, put down a tar paper patch with roofing compound. Then slide in a new shingle and

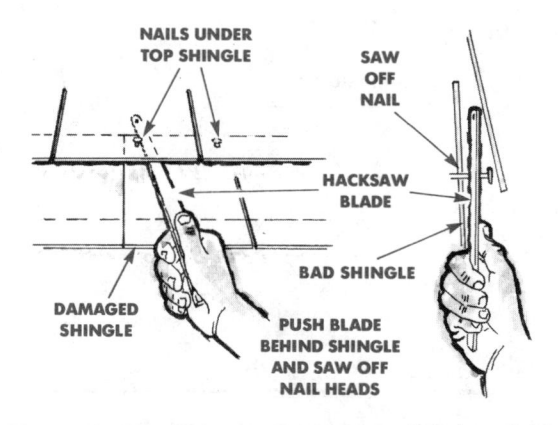

Figure 34-5: Because of the overlapping shingles, it is impossible to remove the nails holding a shingle in place. The easiest way to free the shingle is to cut off the nail heads with a hacksaw blade.

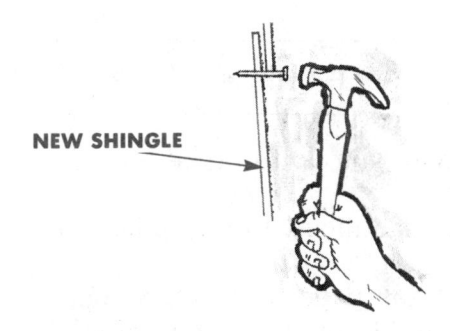

Figure 34-6: Push in the new shingle as far as it will go. Nail just below the shingle above, catching the edge of the shingle with the nail head. Be sure to cement over all nails.

nail just below the butt of the overlapping shingle with rust-resistant nails (figure 34-6). Cement the shingle and the overlapping row above.

Slate or asbestos shingles last as long as the house unless they are broken. A cracked slate can be patched with asphalt emulsion cement. Replace badly damaged slates. Remove the old shingle carefully and nail down two copper strips extending about two inches below the bottom edge of the new shingle (figure 34-7). It is not easy to nail through the slate shingles below. Use one solid blow. Cover each nail head with asphalt roof cement. Slide in the new shingle and turn up the copper strips to hold the shingle in place.

Wood shingles split and warp as they get older. If a wooden shingle is damaged, a tar paper or metal patch under the shingle will often stop the leak. Replace wooden shingles as you would composition ones. Remember that wooden shingles swell, so they must fit loosely between the other shingles. Nail in the new shingle with rust-resistant nails.

Figure 34-7: Slate shingles are removed when they are broken. Nail two strips of sheet copper where the new tile will be placed. Don't tap in the nail; drive it with one hard blow. Then smear large gobs of roof cement over the nails. This will spread out when you press down the new slate and will help hold it in place. Bend up the copper strips. Later snip off the strips along the edge of the slate.

FLAT TILES   **CURVED TILES**

MISSION TILE   **SPANISH TILE**

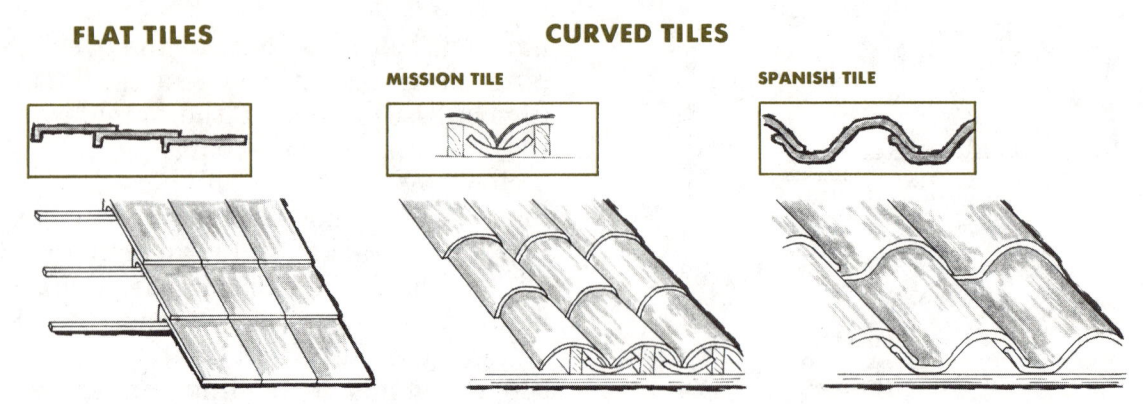

Figure 34-8: Ceramic tiles may be flat or curved. Spanish tile is shaped like an S while mission tile is more like half sections of pipe. On the roof they interlock.

Tile roofs generally suffer only from wind damage. Tiles vary from unglazed red Spanish tiles to glazed Oriental ones. They are curved or flat (figure 34-8). When replacing tiles nail only through the predrilled holes. Avoid placing weight on the tiles or they will crack.

SELF CHECK

1. What can you do to make roof work safer?
2. Why is it difficult to find a leak in a roof?
3. How is tar paper used on a roof?
4. How would you replace a shingle?

ROOFING ACCESSORIES — Unit 35

At first glance, a roof looks pretty plain. But on second look you will see many accessories that require care (figure 35-1). Some of the most common are:
- Flashing
- Roof vents
- Gutters
- Chimney spark guards

Flashing is sheetmetal bent to fill the gaps around chimneys, vent pipes, and valleys where two roof slopes come together (figure 35-2). Remove rusted old flashing and install a new piece.

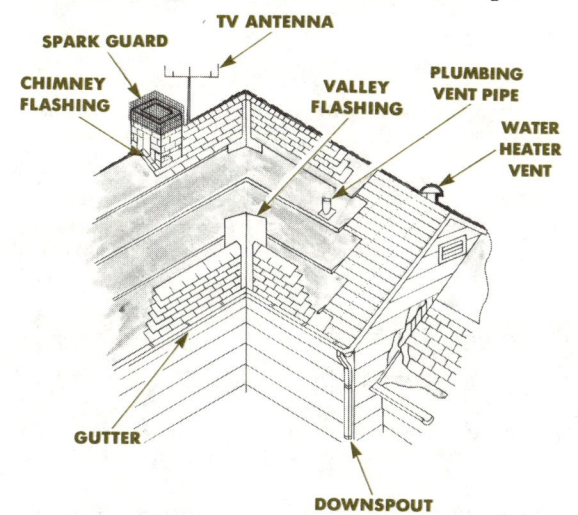

Figure 35-1: Roofs have many accessories that require care.

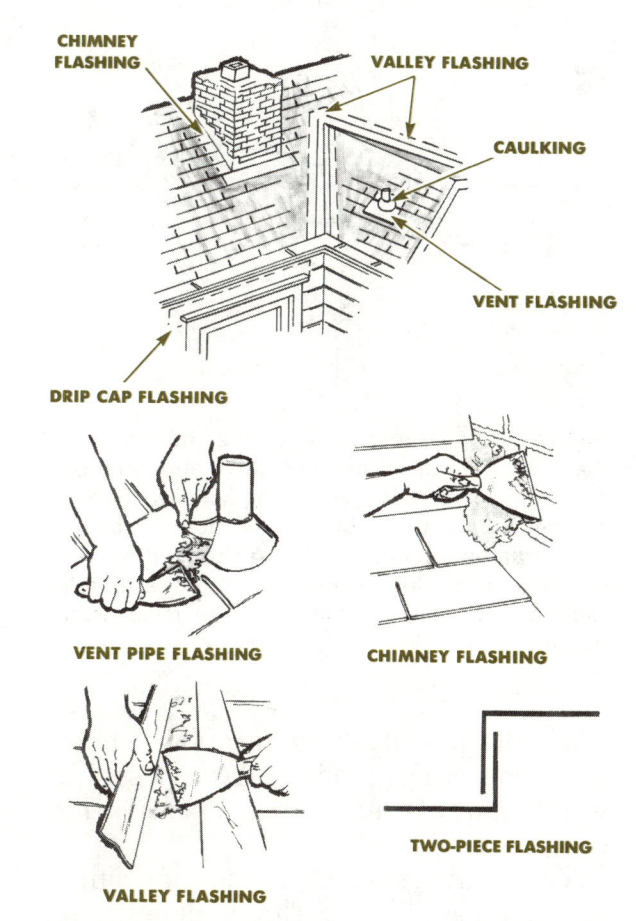

Figure 35-2: Flashing is bent metal that keeps water from seeping into the house. It is bent so that it fits tightly against both surfaces coming together. Some flashing comes in two pieces to assure that water will not come in even when the flashing expands or contracts.

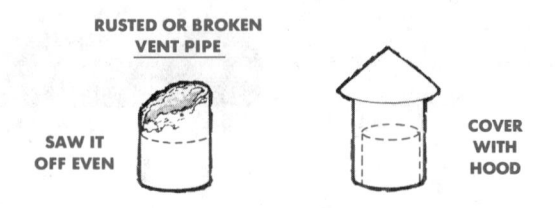

Figure 35-3: Broken or rusted vent pipes are hazardous. Leaves and debris can lodge against them and hot air from the vent could set this material on fire. It is important to keep vents long enough and hoods in good repair.

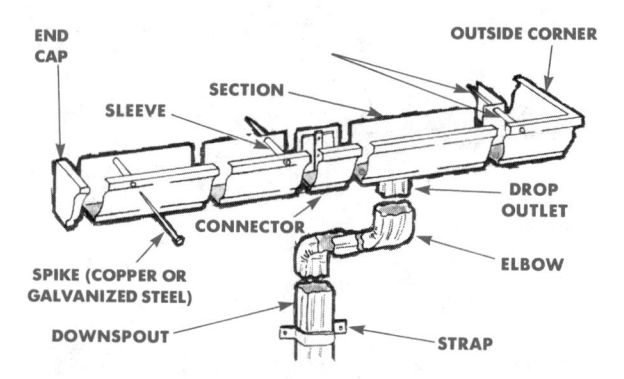

Figure 35-4: Gutters direct water flowing from the roof. They must be kept clean and securely attached to the roof. Pay special attention to cleaning elbows and bends. A clogged downspout can be snaked out. Galvanized gutters are joined with solder; aluminum gutters are held together with mastic cement and aluminum pop rivets.

Tuck the new flashing carefully under the edges of the roofing. Always seal it with asphalt emulsion or calking compound.

There are several kinds of vents. Small pipes, two or three inches, are usually sewer vents. Larger pipes, frequently made of asbestos, are for venting gas or oil water heaters, exhaust hoods over stoves, or bathroom fan exhausts. Vents that discharge hot air must rise four inches above the roof although local codes vary.

Inspect roof vents for rust or clogging. If the vent has a protective hood, keep that in good repair, too. Extend broken or rusted vent pipes by using a slightly larger pipe as a collar. Then add the extension pipe (figure 35-3).

Gutters (figure 35-4) control water running off the roof. They should slope toward the downspout about 1/8 inch per running foot. Clean out gutters at least every six months. Screen guards and leaf strainers will help prevent clogging. Check the hangers and secure or replace them when necessary. Be sure to cover with roof cement any nails that are driven into the roof.

It is a good idea to have a chimney spark guard on every chimney. Spark guards are made of 1/8-inch mesh hardware cloth (figure 35-5). They keep sparks from landing on the roof. Don't use a smaller mesh or it will clog with soot.

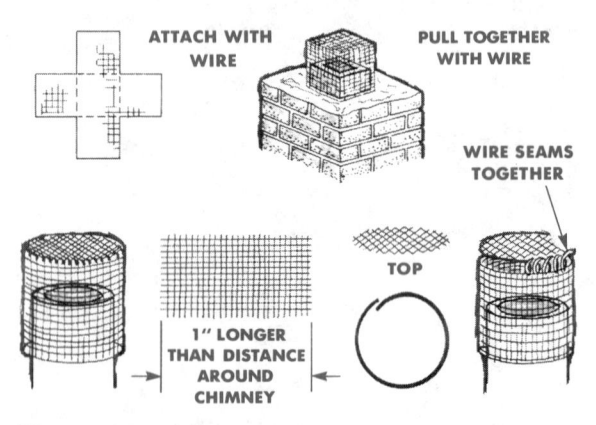

Figure 35-5: Two ways of building spark arresters from hardware cloth. Every chimney should have one.

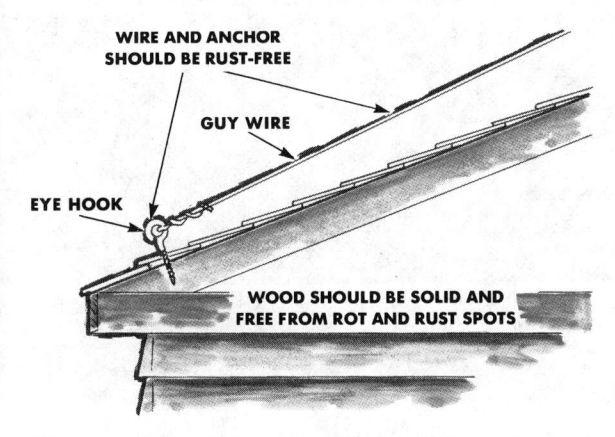

Figure 35-6: When checking anything attached to the roof or eaves, look for rust getting into the wood. Rust can cause a type of rot that weakens wood.

When you are on the roof also check antennas. The wires and anchors should be secure and free from rust. Be sure the roof is solid when the anchors are set (figure 35-6).

SELF CHECK

1. Name at least four pieces of hardware commonly found on roofs.
2. What does flashing do?
3. How can you repair a broken vent pipe?
4. What size hardware cloth should you use for a spark guard?

CONCRETE AND ASPHALT   6

People walk, ride, and play on concrete and asphalt surfaces. Because the greatest use of these products is in floors, slabs, sidewalks, and streets, concrete and asphalt aren't usually considered home repair problems. But almost every house has some cement in or under it. Concrete workers and finishers will always be in demand because cement is useful and durable.

MORTAR AND CONCRETE — Unit 36

Cement means an adhesive that holds things together. Cement is a word that is often used in place of:
- Mortar or
- Concrete

Mortar is usually a mixture of sand and Portland cement used with or instead of lime for greater strength. It is used to cement bricks and tiles together. To prepare mortar, add the correct amount of water and mix (figure 36-1). Mortar works best on a wet surface. Dry brick or block will absorb water from the mortar before it can set properly. Whenever possible, soak the block, brick, or wall to be patched before applying mortar.

When gravel, crushed stone, or some other aggregate is added to sand and Portland cement, it is called concrete (figure 36-2). Concrete can be bought in different sized sacks. When mixed with water, one 80-pound sack of premix will make up an amount that will fill a section 4 feet by 4 feet by 1/2 inch. You

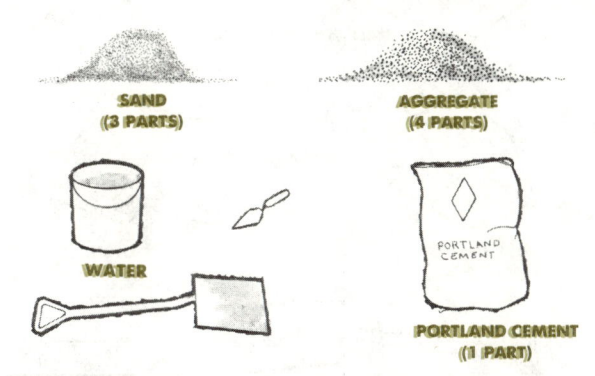

Figure 36-2: Add an aggregate to mortar and you have concrete. Concrete can be mixed in different proportions. One common mixture contains one part Portland cement, three parts sand, four parts aggregate and a little water.

Figure 36-1: Mortar can be mixed in a suitable container by hand. It contains Portland cement, sand and water and sometimes lime in certain proportions.

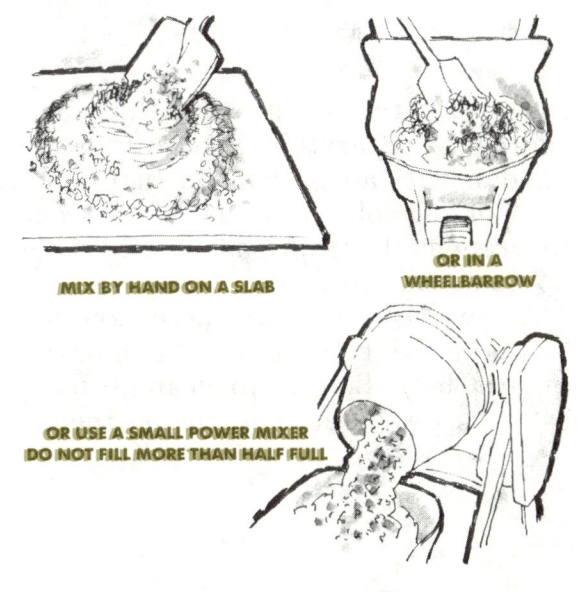

Figure 36-3: Concrete can be mixed in a container such as a pail or a wheelbarrow or on a slab or piece of plywood. You can also use a small power mixer, but do not fill it more than half full or it will not mix properly. Never mix concrete on the ground. The slightest bit of mud weakens the concrete.

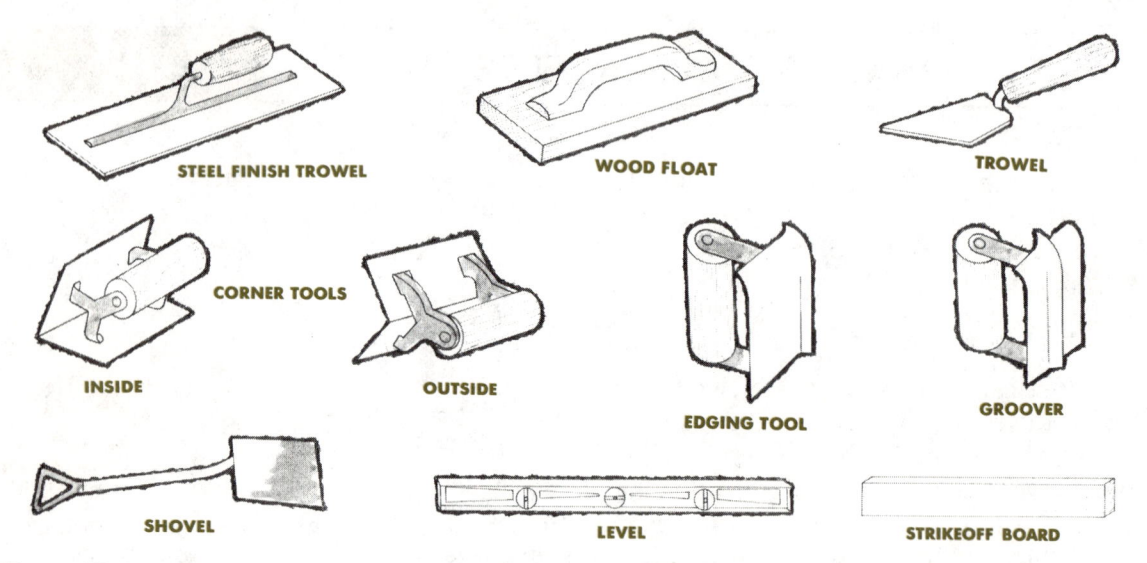

Figure 36-4: Depending on the job, you will need some of these tools for work with mortar or concrete. Always keep tools clean.

can also purchase the sand, lime and aggregate separately and mix it by hand or with a power mixer (figure 36-3). For big jobs it is easiest to order concrete by the truckload already made up and ready to pour.

A few basic tools are necessary for working with concrete or mortar (figure 36-4). Be sure to clean all tools before the concrete hardens on them.

SELF CHECK

1. What is the difference between mortar and cement?
2. How many sacks of premixed concrete will you need to fill two cubic feet?
3. What are two ways of mixing concrete?
4. What basic tools will you need for working with mortar and concrete?

MASONRY REPAIRS   Unit 37

Basic masonry repairs include:
- Filling in dings in floors and driveways
- Replacing a block or brick
- Repointing mortar

To patch concrete first remove all loose material from the old concrete. Use a vacuum cleaner. Then scrub away any oil or grease with hot water and trisodium phosphate (TSP). Use a stiff brush. Protect your hands with rubber gloves.

After the concrete is clean, wet it. Fill in the patch. The best mix for patching concrete is one part Portland cement to three parts fine, clean sand. Add concrete glue to help feather out the edges of your patch and secure it to the old concrete (figure 37-1). Leave a wet rag or gunny sack over the patch for a couple days.

Replace a broken or missing concrete block with the same mix. Chisel the old mortar away. Soak the new block in water for five minutes and wet the blocks around the hole. Trowel in

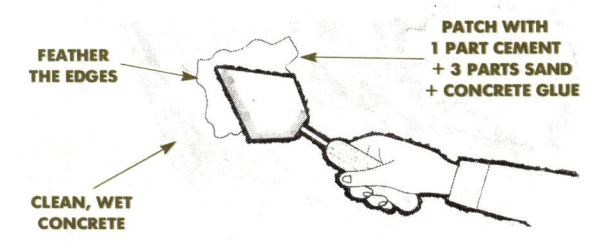

Figure 37-1: To patch concrete, clean and wet the area. Fill in the area and feather the edges so the patch will stick.

Figure 37-2: When you replace a brick or block, trowel in mortar around the opening. Nudge the block in place with the handle of a trowel or a piece of wood.

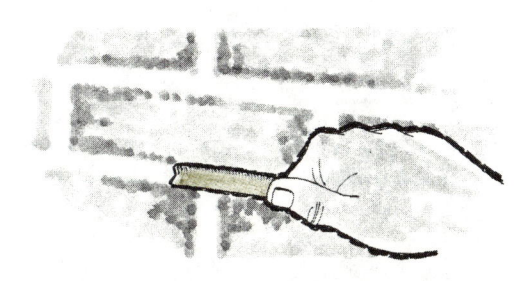

Figure 37-3: Use a finishing tool to finish mortar joints after the mortar begins to harden.

mortar on all sides and set in the new block. You may have to take some mortar out little by little to make the block fit. Keep nudging the block with your trowel handle or a piece of wood (figure 37-2). Don't use a hammer.

Once the block is in place and aligned, tool the joint to match the rest of the wall. If the other joints are tuckpointed (grooved) make the new joint match (figure 37-3). Wipe up any mortar spilled on the face of the block before it hardens.

Replacing a fired (red) brick is the same as a concrete block. But be very careful to match the color or your replacement will stand out.

Try not to spill mortar over the face of the brick. If you do, you can remove the stain with acid and a stiff brush. BE CAREFUL WHEN WORKING WITH ACID. Always add the acid to water. Adding water to acid can cause an explosion. Protect yourself with goggles and rubber gloves. Wear old clothing. Muriatic acid will remove clothes, eyes, and skin faster than it will remove the mortar stain.

Repointing is putting new mortar into joints when the old mortar is falling out. First clean out the crumbling mortar. You can make a tool for this by nailing through a block of wood until the point of the nail extends 1/2 inch (figure 37-4). Slide this point along the joints and you won't dig too deep. Then wet the bricks and flush out loose mortar with a good strong hose jet.

Mix no more mortar than you can use in one hour. If you are repointing a whole wall or chimney, use any color mortar. However, if you are patching only a section, take care to match the color of the old mortar. Don't work with mortar when the temperature is below freezing.

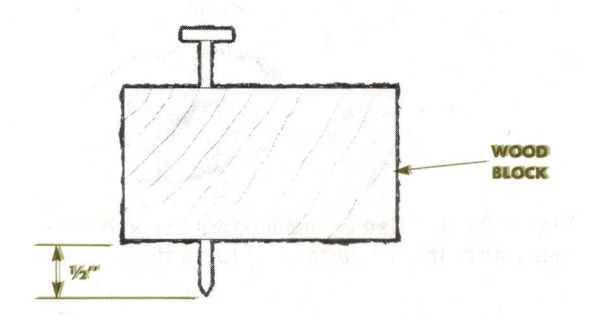

Figure 37-4: You can make a tool to remove old mortar by driving a nail through a block of wood until it extends about ½ inch.

SELF CHECK

1. What safety rules should you follow when working with TSP?
2. What is the best mixture for patching concrete?
3. How should acid be handled?
4. How much mortar should you mix at a time?

POURING CONCRETE Unit 38

Placing concrete is not difficult. Big jobs and little jobs all require the same basic steps:
- Preparing the surface and setting up the forms
- Figuring the amount of concrete you will need
- Pouring and finishing the concrete

The ground under the concrete must be compact and free from standing water and tree roots. Concrete on soft, unpacked ground will crack in a very short time. If drainage is a problem, put down gravel first and compact it.

Close in the area with 2 x 4's (figure 38-1). Drive in a stake about every three feet. The poured concrete is heavy and will press against the forms. So they must be supported to hold up the concrete. Make the forms level or at a slight incline for drainage.

Before you start mixing the concrete, decide how much you will need. A four-inch thick slab is standard, especially in areas where the ground freezes. One 94 lb. sack of premixed concrete will make 1 cubic foot. For a 4-inch slab, you will need 1 sack for every 9 square feet. Multiply the length by the width to see how many square feet are needed. A 4-inch piece that is 3 feet x 5 feet (15 sq. ft.) would require two sacks. Be sure to mix a little more than you think you will need. You can always pour the extra into a mold to make a block or ornamental flower pot (figure 38-2). A light coat of oil on the forms will prevent the cement from sticking.

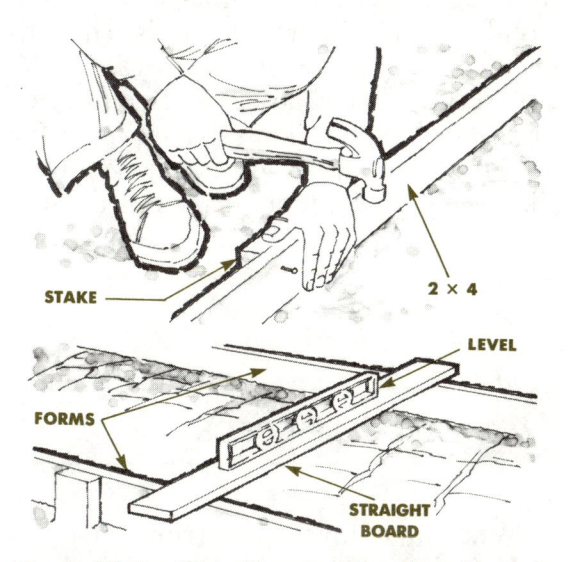

Figure 38-1: When the ground surface is ready, set up forms for the concrete. Nail stakes in place every three feet so the forms will hold up against the weight of the concrete. Place a board across the tops of the forms and check with a level.

Figure 38-2: Excess concrete can be poured into a mold to make blocks or flagstones or even into a can or milk carton to make a planter.

Figure 38-3: Level off the concrete with a straight board. This is called screeding. Don't try to get the surface smooth, just level.

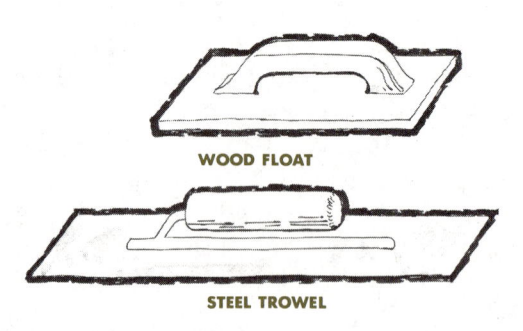

Figure 38-4: When the concrete begins to harden, smooth the surface with a wood float and finish with a steel trowel. Avoid excessive troweling because it weakens the concrete and may make the surface too smooth. Finally, brush for a textured, non-slip surface.

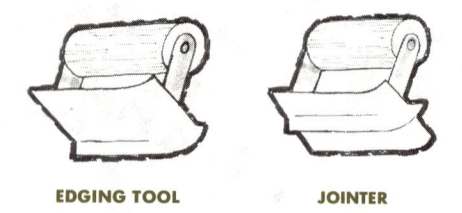

Figure 38-5: Edging and jointing tools give a professional finish to sidewalks and concrete slabs.

Pour the concrete in place. Avoid carrying it and handling it. Fill the form and level off the top by running a board across the top of the forms (figure 38-3).

Slide a shingle or run an edger along the inside of the form boards to work out bubbles and work the gravel in. This will give a better appearance to the edges.

When the concrete begins to set up (20 or 30 minutes) and the water film on top has disappeared, trowel the surface smooth (figure 38-4). Avoid excessive troweling. Place a groove every two or three feet because sooner or later the concrete will crack and the grooves let it crack into neat squares. Use an edger or jointer (figure 38-5) to give a professional look to the grooves and edges and to prevent corners from breaking off. Cover the finished concrete with plastic or wet straw. The concrete will be ready to walk on in two or three days, but don't drive over it for at least a week. Keep heavy vehicles, like trucks, off for at least ten days.

SELF CHECK

1. Why must forms be strong?
2. How far will a sack of premixed concrete go?
3. Why are grooves placed in concrete?
4. How long does it take for the concrete to thoroughly set?

BASEMENTS   Unit 39

Basements are simply concrete boxes set in the ground. In dry parts of the country, seasonal rains may flood a basement. In wetter areas, ground water may keep the basement damp all year. Three common basement problems are:
- Dampness
- Cracks
- Holes

New basements are usually waterproofed with asphalt or plastic or a combination of the two (figure 39-1).

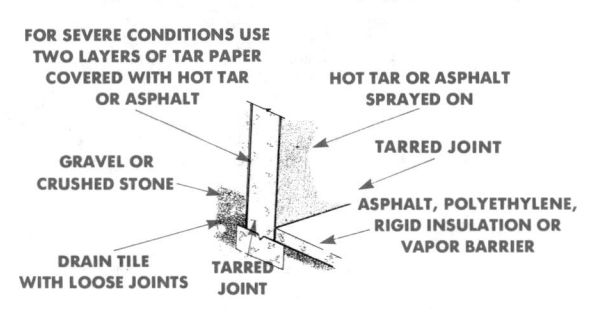

Figure 39-1: New basements are usually waterproofed with asphalt or plastic or a combination of the two.

If your basement has water seeping through the pores of the wall, the best solution is to waterproof it from the outside. To do this, dig down along the outside of the basement wall. Clean and coat the area with an asphalt preparation (figure 39-2). Another solution is to lay a drainage channel along the basement wall at ground level. This channel should slant about 1/8 inch per running foot (figure 39-3). The wider the channel, the more it will protect the basement wall against seepage.

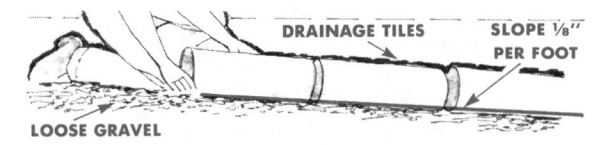

Figure 39-3: Two kinds of drainage protection are possible for a basement. One is to lay a drain at the bottom of the wall in loose gravel. This carries off water before water pressure accumulates. Another solution is to build up the soil around the building so it will carry off the surface water before it soaks into the ground.

Figure 39-2: The best barrier is applied to the outside of the basement wall.

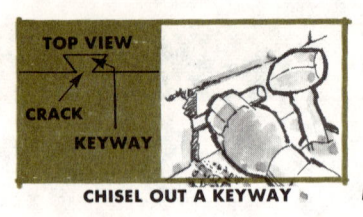

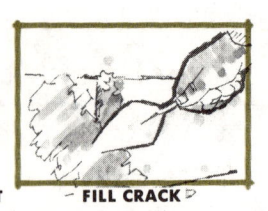

Figure 39-4: Shape a keyway with a chisel so the narrow end is at the front. This keeps the patch from falling out. Mix mortar or epoxy and force it deep into the crack. After about a half hour use a wet trowel to smooth the patch.

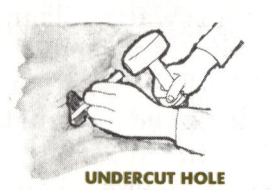

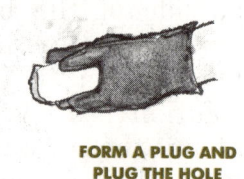

Figure 39-5: When the hole is wet use hydraulic cement. Undercut the hole. Mix the cement and form a plug. When the plug begins to harden, force it into the hole.

If the water can't be stopped from the outside and is caused by a crack, use a wire brush to clean all loose material out of the crack. Shape the crack into a keyway with a chisel (figure 39-4). Fill the keyway with mortar or epoxy cement. Mortar is made by mixing one part mortar cement with three parts fine, sharp sand (beach sand won't cling) and a little water or glue. Mortar shrinks when it dries, so, for a final waterproofing, cover the mortar with epoxy cement. You may fill the entire crack with epoxy cement if the wall is dry. Epoxy works better than mortar but costs more.

If the hole must be filled while it is wet, use a fast-setting hydraulic cement. Mix it according to the directions on the package and roll it into a cigar shape. As soon as the cement starts to harden, force it into the hole. Smooth it with a trowel and hold it in place until it finishes setting (figure 39-5).

Paint damp basement walls with dry powder. Dry powder is a concrete-base paint that mixes with water and helps seal the pores of the concrete. You may also use latex paint.

If all of this fails you may have to learn to live with periodic or constant flooding. Capping the floor with cement and inclining it to the center of the basement, will create a drain channel which can be run to a sewer drain. If the basement floor is below sewer level, end the channel at a hole in the floor called a sump. A pump connected to the sump will lift water to the nearest sewer drain or the outside.

SELF CHECK

1. What is the single biggest basement problem?
2. What is the best way to waterproof a basement?
3. How do you plug a wet, leaking hole?
4. What types of paint stick to wet cement?

FURNITURE MAINTENANCE

7

At one time most furniture was made of wood. Today many furniture items are made of other materials such as various kinds of plastic. In any case, it is usually less expensive to repair or refinish a piece of furniture than it is to replace it. Outdoor furniture probably gets more wear and tear than indoor furniture, but it is often easy to repair. Sometimes a few minutes of your time will extend the life of a chair or table by several years.

Unit 40 FURNITURE REPAIR

Besides normal wear and tear, hot, dry air can cause wooden furniture to shrink and come apart. The four most common furniture problems are:
- Wood shrinkage
- Warping
- Worn seating
- Scrapes and scratches

If table or chair legs begin to come unglued, finish knocking them apart with a soft wooden block and a mallet (figure 40-1). Remove old glue with a dull knife or hook scraper and sandpaper. Scrape glue out of the holes, too. Remove only the old glue. If you sand off any wood, the joints will be too loose.

Use white vinyl glue and reassemble the chair or table. Wipe up any spills or runs before they dry. Then, with rope or a webbed clamp, clamp the legs

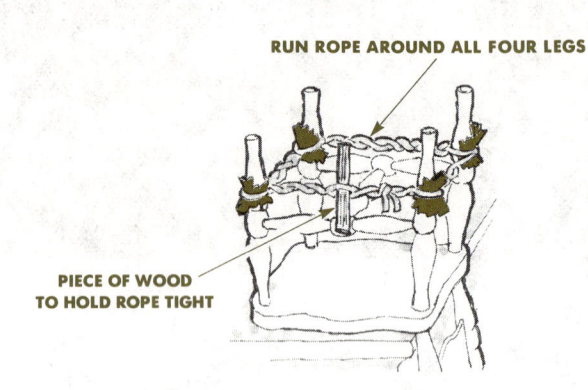

Figure 40-2: Winding a doubled piece of rope between chair legs produces a gentle vise effect. Don't twist too much or the chair will break. Turn the rope just tight enough for everything to stay in place. Glued joints should always be clamped because furniture parts tend to lean or bend in the wrong directions.

in place until the glue dries (figure 40-2).

A warped table top can be straightened. Warping is caused by uneven drying. First strip off the paint and varnish. Paint remover is dangerous. Wear rubber gloves and follow the manufacturer's instructions carefully.

Next soak the wood by piling wet newspaper, wet sawdust, or wet towels on top for four or five days. When the wood is soaked through, remove the newspaper, sawdust, or towels and place weights or clamps on the warped boards (figure 40-3). When everything is clamped or weighted down, leave it in a warm dry room for a few days. Move the clamps each day to help the wood dry evenly and prevent cracking.

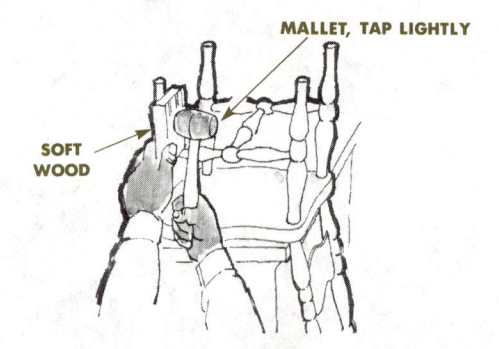

Figure 40-1: With a block of soft wood and a mallet, take apart loose wooden furniture for regluing. Tap a little on each joint. Make sure all joints are loose or you might end up breaking something.

Furniture Repair 113

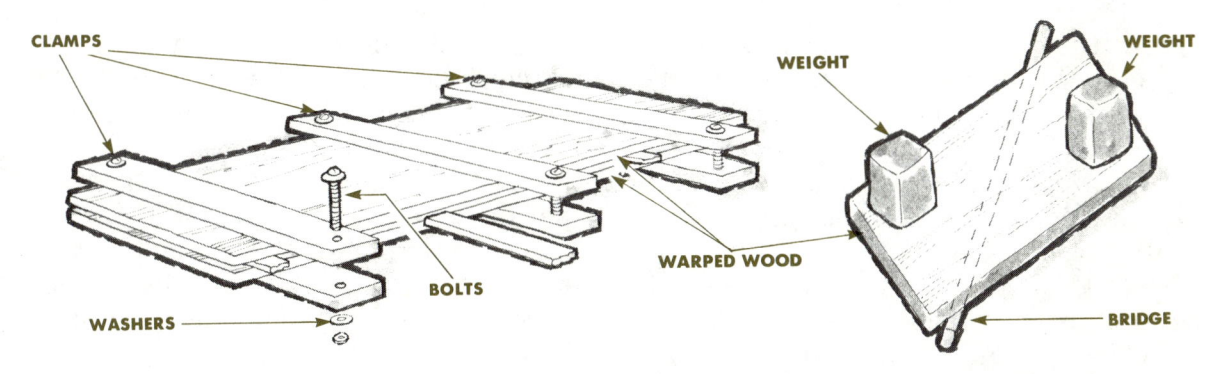

Figure 40-3: To straighten out warped boards, add moisture. Clean off the board and clamp it down for several days.

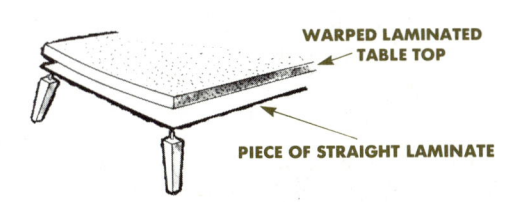

Figure 40-4: If laminated furniture warps, wait until the weather is right and it will straighten out again. While it is straight, glue another piece of laminate to the bottom side to hold it.

As soon as the boards have dried straight, refinish BOTH SIDES to keep more moisture from entering or leaving the wood.

This method will not straighten laminated wood. Wait until the weather changes and the laminated piece will straighten by itself. When it does, glue another piece of scrap laminate on the underside. It will remain straight (figure 40-4).

A kitchen chair seat or back is held on with only two or four screws. The cushion is usually made of foam or cotton batting covered with cloth or plastic folded over a piece of plywood (figure 40-5). Replace old cotton bat-

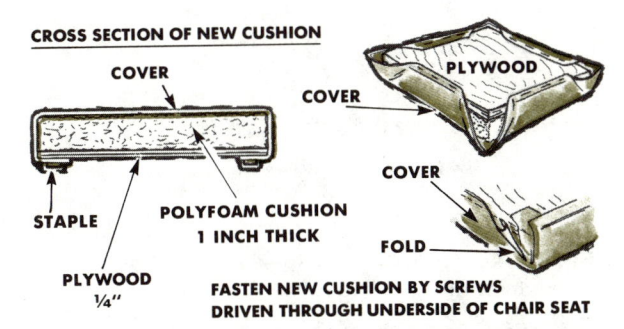

Figure 40-5: To improve kitchen chairs, replace the old cotton batting in the seats with polyfoam cushioning. If necessary replace the covering too. Fold it carefully over the foam and plywood. The hardest part is folding the material properly.

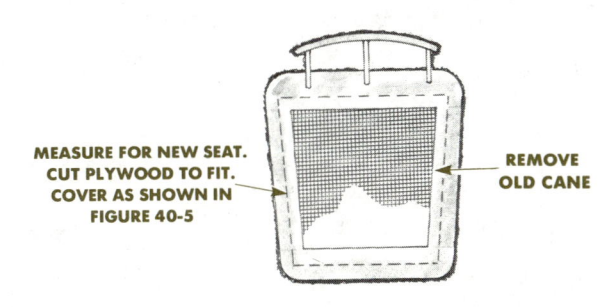

Figure 40-6: Recaning a chair is expensive. One solution is to make a plywood and polyfoam cushion to fit the chair seat.

ting with foam cut to size. Polyfoam is softer and lasts longer than cotton batting without getting lumpy or hard.

Cane bottom chairs can be modernized and made more comfortable by removing the cane part of the seat. Cover the seat with a cushion of plywood, polyfoam and a cover of plastic or cloth (figure 40-6).

To fix a small scratch on furniture use a crayon-like touchup stick (figure 40-7). They come in various shades to match different finishes. Sometimes iodine or shoe dye will work too. If the crack is deep, fill with wood putty. When it dries, rub stick shellac over the area. Stick shellac is applied with a spatula knife heated over an alcohol lamp. Finally, rub with felt or fine steel wool (figure 40-8). Sometimes toothpaste will rub out fine scratches.

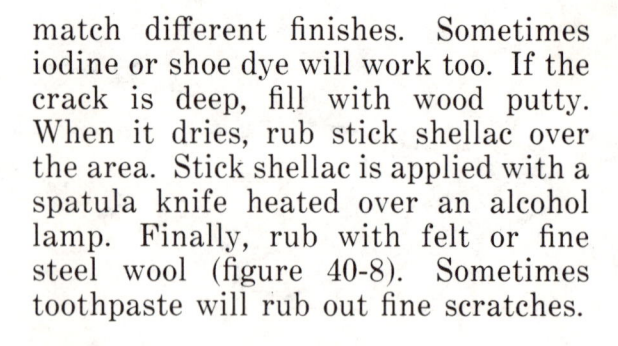

Figure 40-7: Cover hairline scratches with a touchup stick, iodine or shoe dye.

FILL WITH WOOD PUTTY   COVER WITH STICK SHELLAC   RUB SMOOTH

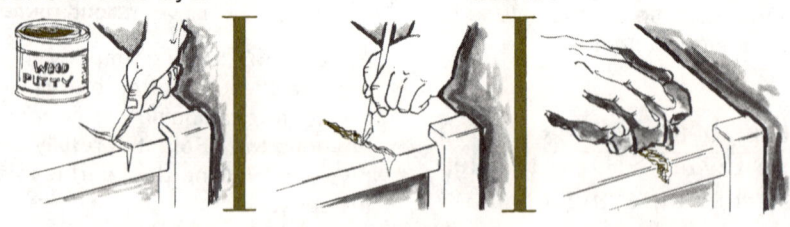

Figure 40-8: Fill deeper scratches and gouges with wood putty. Cover with stick shellac. Finally rub it down with a felt pad or extra fine steel wool.

SELF CHECK

1. What precautions should you take when working with stripper?
2. How would you repair a loose chair leg?
3. Why does wood warp?
4. Why should polyfoam be used to replace cotton batting in chair seats?

REFINISHING FURNITURE — Unit 41

Furniture refinishing includes three basic steps:
- Removing the old finish
- Preparing the surface
- Applying the new finish

Sometimes the old furniture finish doesn't really need to be stripped off. A good washing with TSP will get the grease off. Then roughen the surface with fine sandpaper or steel wool and coat it with varnish or clear lacquer (figure 41-1). Do not apply lacquer over varnish, paint, or enamel. It will remove the finish just as a stripper would.

There is no way to blend a new finish with an old finish. If the furniture is badly worn, you will have to strip the finish off the entire piece. You can do this by scraping or sanding for a long time. Or you can use chemical compounds, which work much faster (figure 41-2). Chemical strippers soften and loosen the paint quickly, and when the

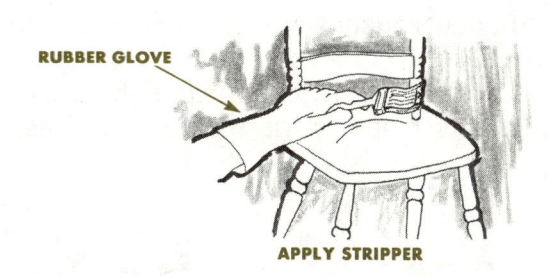

Figure 41-2: Chemical strippers will remove old paint, varnish or lacquer quickly. Follow instructions carefully. If the stripper needs to be neutralized be sure to do so at the proper time. Handle chemicals with care.

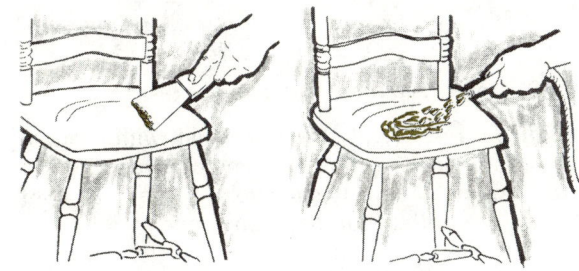

Figure 41-3: Scrape off loose paint with a putty knife or spray off with a garden hose. After the wood is dry, sand down the raised grain.

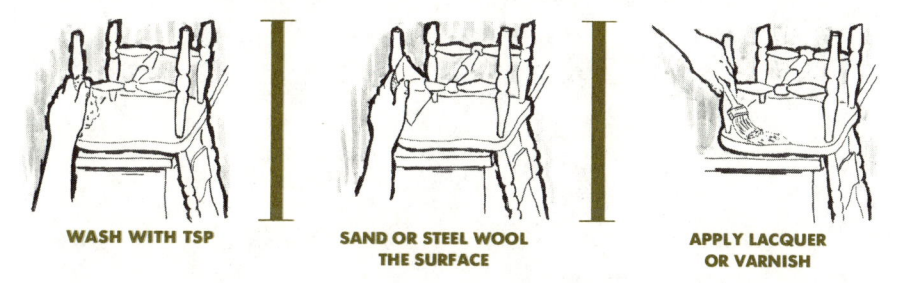

Figure 41-1: Sometimes you can apply a new coat of finish without stripping the piece of furniture. Clean the surface and sand it lightly so the new finish will stick. Apply a new coat of varnish or lacquer. Do not use lacquer over varnish or paint or it will act like a stripper and cause the finish below to soften and bubble up.

paint is dissolved they will begin to work on the wood and glue. For this reason, you must apply a neutralizer as soon as the last coat of paint or varnish is soft. Then rinse off both stripper and neutralizer along with the old finish (figure 41-3).

Always handle chemical substances such as stripper with great care. Wear rubber gloves and read all instructions carefully before you begin to work.

After the furniture is stripped to the original wood, give it time to dry. Then sand to even off the raised grain.

If you want to change the color of the wood, add wood stain. Follow up with varnish or lacquer. Instead you may want to apply paint or enamel (figure 41-4). Refer to Units 23, 25, and 26 for more information on painting.

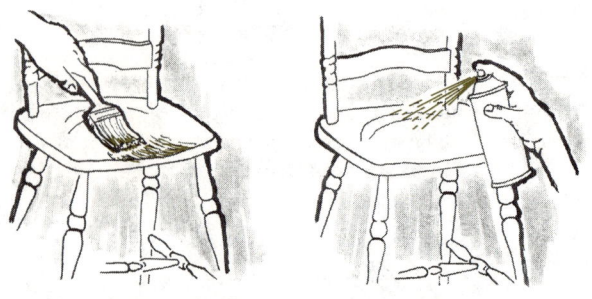

APPLY NEW FINISH WITH BRUSH OR SPRAY

Figure 41-4: Apply the new finish with a brush or spray can. Practice on some old wood before you begin. Apply finish evenly. Several light coats are better than one heavy one.

SELF CHECK

1. What are two ways to strip old paint or varnish off furniture?
2. What will happen if you don't neutralize paint stripper?
3. Can you strip bad sections of furniture and let the good parts go?
4. What are some methods of finishing wood furniture?

OUTDOOR FURNITURE Unit 42

Outdoor furniture is usually made of metal or wood like redwood which resists rot. Common outdoor furniture repairs include:
- Refinishing wood or metal
- Repairing breaks
- Replacing canvas or webbing

Outdoor furniture needs a good protective finish. Use exterior paints or enamels. If the metal has begun to rust, clean it thoroughly. Then prime the surface with an anti-rust primer. Use undercoating on wood surfaces.

Often a "sawbuck" chair or table will break where the legs cross. Join the pieces again with a splint glued on and reinforced with several screws (figure 42-1). The new joint will probably be stronger than the original piece.

A director's chair comes apart easily (figure 42-2). While it's apart sand and refinish it. Use the old canvas back and seat as a pattern for the new ones.

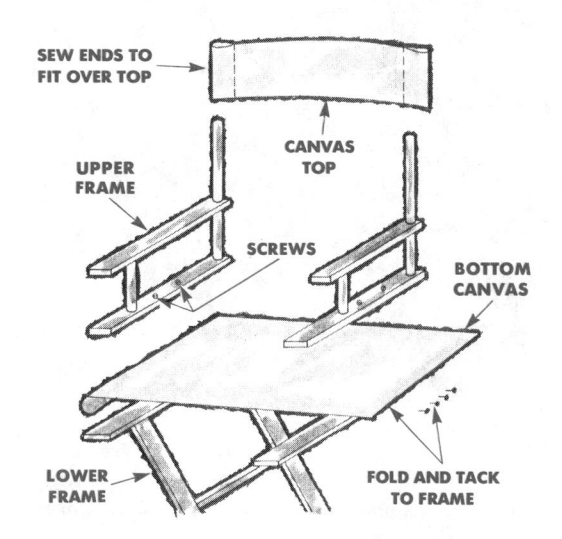

Figure 42-2: A director's chair comes apart easily for repair. Refinish the wood parts. Cut new canvas patterned on the old pieces.

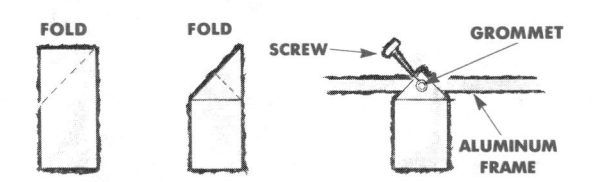

Figure 42-3: On a webbed chair, fold over the end of each strap twice and insert a grommet before attaching the webbing to the frame with a screw. This will reinforce the hole and keep the webbing from pulling out the first time you sit down.

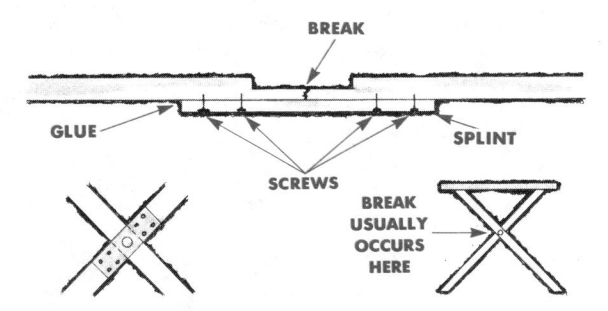

Figure 42-1: If the wood breaks on a patio chair or table, a good way to repair is to glue the piece together with a reinforcing splint over the break. Use screws to hold the splint in place.

Aluminum frame chairs can be recovered with webbing. Save the old grommets and screws. Be sure the chair is fully unfolded when rewebbing. Fold the end of the webbing over twice (figure 42-3) and puncture the end with

Figure 42-4: Plastic tubing or cord wrapped around an aluminum frame makes a durable, weatherproof chair.

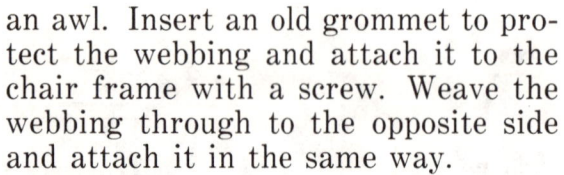

Figure 42-5: With cord and canvas chairs, all you have to remember is to knot the end of the cord.

an awl. Insert an old grommet to protect the webbing and attach it to the chair frame with a screw. Weave the webbing through to the opposite side and attach it in the same way.

Some chairs have frames wound with plastic tubing (figure 42-4). This plastic is very durable. Cord and canvas chairs are easy to repair (figure 42-5).

SELF CHECK

1. Why is redwood used for patio furniture?
2. How would you repair a "sawbuck" table or chair?
3. How would you measure the canvas to fit a director's chair?
4. How is webbing replaced on lawn chairs?

GLOSSARY

AC: Alternating current. In the United States, AC is usually 110 volts, 60 hertz.

Ballast: A small part in a fluorescent light fixture shaped like a flashlight battery. When it wears out, the fluorescent light will not work.

Baseboard: A trim around the bottom of a wall which keeps feet, vacuum cleaners from damaging the wall surface.

Breaker: (Circuit breaker is the full name.) A breaker acts like a fuse to cut off electricity when wires are overloaded. A circuit breaker can be reset after it cools off.

Building code: A set of rules and regulations relating to safety, material and construction standards. If a house is not up to code the city can make you tear it down.

Casement window: A steel-framed window that opens with a crank.

Cement: Another name for glue. Portland cement is mixed with sand and gravel to make concrete. Mixed with sand or sometimes lime, it makes mortar.

Circuit tester: An electrical device which tells if current is flowing. Often consists of just a light bulb and two wires.

Concrete: A hardened mixture of Portland cement and aggregate.

Conductor: A substance that carries electricity. Metals, impure water, human bodies are all excellent conductors.

Coupling: A connecting sleeve with internal threads for joining two lengths of pipe.

DC: Direct Current. Batteries and generators produce DC.

Downspout: A vertical drainpipe to carry water from gutters to the ground. Sometimes round but usually rectangular in cross section.

Drywall: A sandwiched cardboard and gypsum panel.

Duct: Usually a rectangular sheetmetal passageway for heat and air conditioning. Ductwork is usually concealed between floors and seen only where it ends at a register.

Face plate: The metal plate on the edge of a door through which the bolt and latch extend.

Faucet washer: A small round plastic or rubber part which is usually first to wear out. Replacing the washer fixes most leaks.

Finish nail: A nail with a very small head. Use it with a nail set and drive the head below the surface. Putty over and the nail's invisible.

Flashing: Sheet metal used to seal the joint between a roof and anything that comes through it, such as a vent, chimney, or skylight.

Flux: Acids or salts used to clean metal and make solder flow.

Fuse: A strip of metal that melts at a certain temperature, thus shutting down an electrical circuit before the wire can get hot somewhere else and start a fire.

Galvanized: Coated with zinc (usually iron or steel).

Gasket: A piece of soft material used to seal irregularities and prevent leaks between two hard surfaces.

Glazier's points: Small sheetmetal triangles used to hold glass while the putty sets.

Glazing: The art of installing window glass.

Grommet: A metal, plastic, or leather reinforcement to keep a hole in woven material from raveling and becoming larger.

Ground: Electrically, a ground is the common return line for all circuits.

Grout: Usually a hard, white cement used for fixing ceramic tile.

Insulator: A nonconductor used to keep electricity from leaking.

Kilowatt hour (kwh): Measurement of electricity. The equivalent of one thousand watts for an hour or one watt for a thousand hours.

Molding: A decorative strip between wall and ceiling.

Mortar: A sand and Portland cement or lime mixture for joining brick.

Nipple: A short piece of pipe with external threads at both ends. The opposite of a coupling.

Outlet receptacle: A place where electricity can be tapped from the circuits within the walls of a house.

Primer: A first coat of paint to seal pores in wood or metal. Usually a cheaper and less colorful kind of paint than the finish coat.

Putty: Putty is a mixture of some hardening oil and a filler-like clay.

Radiator: A device for piping heat from a distant source into a room. Most radiators are heated with steam but some use hot water.

Reducer: A threaded casting for joining two different sizes of pipe.

Relief valve: A safety device to prevent hot water tank explosions.

Sash: The frame around a window.

Shim: A piece of any material inserted between two other parts to keep them the proper distance apart.

Single Pole Switch: A single pole, single throw switch, abbreviated SPST, is the simplest kind and opens or closes a circuit in a single conductor.

Solder: A metal used in a melted condition to join other metals. Soft solder is usually a 50-50 mix of lead and tin. It will not stick unless you flux and clean the metals first.

Spackle: Used to fill small dents in walls or ceilings.

Splice: Any of several different ways of twisting wires together.

Starter: Used to turn on some fluorescent lights. Others don't need one.

Strike plate: Plate in the jamb of the door which holds the latch and bolt when the door is closed. The strike plate must align with the face plate in the door.

Sump: A sump is a hole in the lowest part of a basement floor where water collects. A sump pump keeps the basement dry.

Thermostat: Automatic control which turns a heating or cooling device off at a preset temperature.

Threshold: The bottom part of a door jamb.

Transformer: A device used to change electrical voltage.

Trap: Goosenecked pipe under a sink, bath, or other water fixture. Prevents sewer gas from backing up into house. Traps should always have water in them.

Trisodium phosphate: (Abbreviated TSP.) A strong chemical cleaner for walls before painting. Use gloves. It removes skin.

Underwriters knot: Used to keep cords from tearing loose from small appliances.

Union: A pipe joint which lets pipe be taken apart in the middle without twisting either piece.

Vent: A pipe through the roof to prevent drains from airlocking.

INDEX

A

Acid, 106
Air conditioning, 57
Alternating current (AC), 9
Antennas, 101
Asphalt, 109
Auger (plumber's snake), 41, 48, 50-51

B

Ballast, fluorescent light, 28-29
Baseboards, 60, 80-81
Basements, 109-110
Bolts, 8
Bowl, toilet, 38, 41
Boxes, electrical, 17, 19
Brads, 6
Brick, 105, 106
Brushes, 71-73
Building codes, 33

C

Cane chairs, 113-114
Canvas chair, 117
Caps, 44
Carpeting, 83
Casement windows, 87
Ceilings, 59-60
Cement, 103
Chair cushioning, 113-114
Chair repair, 112, 117-118
Chimes, 24, 25
Circuit breaker, 11
Circuit tester, 11, 12, 17, 26
Clamp, electrical, 23
Clamp-on plug, 13
Cleanout plug, 49, 50-51
Compression faucet, 35-37
Concrete, 102-108
Conductors, electrical, 10

Connectors, electrical, 23
Copper tubing, 42-43, 45-46
Cords, electrical, 15-16
Countersinking, 7
Couplings, 44
Current, 9

D

Dents, wall, 61
Dimmer switch, 20
Doorbells, 24-26
Door frames, 91-92
Drain pipes, 50
Drilling, 7
Drywall, 59-60

F

Faceplate, door, 94
Fasteners, 6-8
Faucets, 35-37
Finish nails, 6-7
Fire, 65
Fittings, pipe, 43-44
Flames, 2
Flashing, 99-100
Float, wooden, 108
Floor coverings, 83-84
Fluorescent lights, 27-29

E

Electrical safety, 10-12
Electricity, 2, 9-31
Electrolysis, 43
Electromagnet, 24
Ells, 44
Enamel, 70
Epoxy, 110
Eye protection, 4, 5

Flux, 23
Forms, concrete, 107
Frames, window, 85-87
Furniture, 111-118
    outdoor, 117-118
Fuses, 10-12

G

Gage, screw, 7
Galvanizing, 42-43
Gasket, toilet, 41
Glass,
    measuring, 88
    scoring, 89
Glazier's points, 89, 90
Glazing, 88-90
Gutters, 100

H-K

Hardware, door, 93-94
Heaters, water, 52-54
Heating, 55-57
Hinges, 93-94
Holes, wall, 61-62
Hot, electrically, 10
Hot water heating, 55
Insulators, electrical, 10
Joining pipe, 45-47
Keyway, 110
Kilowatt-hour (kwh), 30-31

L

Lacquer, 70
Latches, door, 94
Leaks,
    basement, 109
    faucet, 35-37
    roof, 95-96
    steam heat, 56
    toilet, 39-40
    water heater, 53

Leveling concrete, 108
Linoleum, 83

M
Main switch, 11
Masonry, 105-106
Mechanical connectors, 23
Meter, electrical, 30-31
Molding, 60, 80
Mortar, 103-104, 110
Motors, heater, 57

N-O
Nails, 6-7
  drywall, 59
  finish, 6-7
  pops, 61-62
Nipple connector, 44
Nuts, 8
Outlet receptacles, 17-19

P
Pads, paint, 73
Paint,
  applying, 71-75
  mixing, 69-70
Paint safety, 64-66
Painting drywall, 60
Paneling, 60, 80-81
Pigtail splice, 21
Pilot light, heater, 53-54
Pipe,
  black iron, 42
  clay sewer, 42
  copper tubing, 42-43
  galvanized, 42
  plastic, 42-43
  sewer, 50-51
Pipe fittings, 43-44
Pipes, joining, 45-47
Plastic cement, 47
Plastic pipe, 42-43
  joining, 46-47
Plastic trap, 49
Plug,
  cleanout, 44, 49, 50-51
  electrical, 13-14
Plumbing, 32-57
Plumbing safety, 33-34
Plunger,
  doorbell, 26
  plumbing, 48
Priming, 68, 78, 117
Propane torch, 45-46
Push button, doorbell, 24, 25
Putty glazier's, 89, 90

R
Radiators, 55, 56
Rapid-start fluorescent fixture, 27

Reamer, faucet, 37
Reducer fittings, 44
Refinishing furniture, 115-116
Reseating tool, 37
Rollers, paint, 73
Roofs, 95-98
  accessories, 99-101
Rooter (power auger), 51

S
Safety, 2
  chemical mixing, 106
  electrical, 10-12
  paint, 64-66
  plumbing, 33-34
  roof, 95
Safety glasses, 4
Sanding furniture, 116
Sash cord, 86
Scratches, furniture, 114
Screeding, 108
Screws, 7
  drywall, 59
Screw gage, 7
Sealing doors, 92
Seams, wallcovering, 79
Seat dresser, 37
Sediment in water heater, 52-53
Shingles, 96-97
Single pole single throw (SPST)
     switch, 20
Sink traps, 48-49
Sockets,
  electrical, 17
  lamp, 16
Soldering, 23, 45-46
Spark guards, chimney, 100
Splices, wire, 21-23
Spray painting, 65-66, 74-75
Stain, wood, 116
Starter, fluorescent light, 28
Starter-type fluorescent light, 27-29
Steam heat, 55-56
Steamer, wallpaper, 78
Stops,
  door, 91
  window, 85-86
Strike plate, door, 94
Stripper, chemical, 115
Structural maintenance, 82-121
Structural settling, 87
Sump pump, 110
Switches, 17, 19-20
  doorbell, 24
  main, 11

T
Tacks, 6
Tank, toilet, 38, 39

  repair kit, 40
Tap splice, 21, 22
Tape, drywall, 62
Thermostat, 55
Thinner, paint, 64-65
Tile,
  floor, 83-84
  roof, 98
  wall, 62-63
Toilets, 38-41
Tools,
  concrete, 108
  hand, 2
  power, 2, 5
  wallpapering, 77
Tool safety, 5, 33, 34
Transformer, 24-25
Traps, sink, 48-49
Trim, wall, 80-81
Trisodium phosphate (TSP), 67, 105, 115
Troweling cement, 108
Tubing, copper, 42-43
  joining, 45-47

U-V
Underwriters knot, 13, 14
Union fitting, 44
Valve,
  float, 38-39, 40
  flush, 38-39, 40
  pressure relief, 53
  seat, 37
Varnish, 70
Ventilation, 65
Vent pipes, 50
Vents, 100

W
Wall coverings, 76-79
Wall finishing, 58-81
Wallpaper, 60, 63
Walls,
  preparing to paint, 67-68
  repairing, 61-63
Warm air heat, 57
Warping, 86, 112-113
  doors, 91
Washerless faucet, 37
Water heaters, 52-54
Waterproofing, 109-110
Weather stripping, 91
Webbing, chair, 117-118
Western Union splice, 21, 22
Window frames, 85-87
Wire, 15
Wired plug, 13
Wood stain, 116
Wrenches, 34